Table of Contents

CHAPTER ONE: INTRODUCTION TO THE HOSPITALITY INDUSTRY	**11**
1. The Evolution of Hospitality: From Ancient Times to Modern Era	11
2. Disputes in the Ancient Hospitality Industry	12
I. Disagreements and Conflicts in the Ancient Greek Society	*12*
II. Roman Empire Drama: Ancient Times' Turmoil	*13*
3. The Rise of Hospitality as a Lucrative Industry	13
CHAPTER TWO: CHALLENGES IN THE HOSPITALITY INDUSTRY	**16**
1. Complexity of Operations: Guest Needs Across Departments	16
2. Transition from Transactional to Relationship Marketing	16
3. Impact of Social Media and Digital Platforms: The Double-Edged Sword	18
CHAPTER THREE: LITIGATION IN THE HOSPITALITY INDUSTRY	**20**
1. The Rise of Complaints and Disputes: Hotel, Guest, and the Travel Agent	20
2. The Rise of Complaints and Disputes: Hotels and Employees	20
3. The Rise of Disputes and Legal Cases	21
4. Lengthy Procedures and Associated Costs	23
5. The Need for Alternative Dispute Resolution (ADR)	24
CHAPTER FOUR: THE ROLE OF ADR IN THE HOSPITALITY INDUSTRY	**27**
1. The Impact of Digital Age on Customer Feedback	27
2. The Importance of ADR in the Hospitality Industry	29
3. Examples of ADR in the Hospitality Industry	30
CHAPTER FIVE : NAVIGATING DISPUTES IN MODERN HOSPITALITY	**33**
Internal:	33
1. Employee Relations	33
1.2. Work-related Grievances	*34*
1.3. Misunderstandings	*35*
2. Management-Stakeholder Relations	35

2.1 Stakeholders Success strategies. *35*

2.2 Financial Matters. *37*

2.3 Business Direction. *38*

EXTERNAL. 38

1. . Owner-Operator Hotel Management Agreements.. 38

1.1. Overview of Owner-Operator Hotel Management Agreements. *38*

1.2. Common Disputes in Owner-Operator Hotel Management Agreements. *39*

1.2.1. Disagreements over financial responsibilities. *40*

1.2.2. Disputes regarding property maintenance and renovations. *40*

1.2.3. Conflicts related to staffing and employment. *41*

1.2.4. Disagreements on marketing and branding strategies *42*

2. . Best Practices for Avoiding and Resolving Disputes 43

2.1. Clear and comprehensive contract drafting. *43*

2.2. Regular communication and performance monitoring. *43*

2.3. Establishing dispute resolution procedures upfront *44*

2.4. Seeking legal advice and counsel *44*

2.5. Maintaining a cooperative and collaborative relationship *44*

3. . Resolution Mechanisms for Disputes. 45

1.1. Negotiation *46*

1.2. Litigation *46*

1.3. Arbitration. *47*

1.4. Mediation *48*

CHAPTER SIX: UNDERSTANDING MEDIATION   51

1. . The Rise of Mediation.. 51

2. . Mediation In the Modern Era.. 52

3. . Challenges and Limitations of Mediation in the Hospitality Industry. 53

Examples of Mediation in the Hospitality Industry. *54*

Hotel Owner and Franchisee Dispute: 54

Restaurant Operator and Hotel Manager Conflict: 54

Condo-Hotel Developer and Unit Purchasers: 55

Maintaining Voluntary Participation: 55

4. Benefits of Mediation in the Hospitality Industry 55

5. Mediation vs. Litigation: A Comparison 56

6. The Role of Mediators in Resolving Disputes 58

7. Mediation Training and Certification for Hospitality Professionals 58

8. Mediation Policies and Procedures in the Hospitality Industry 59

9. Mediation Ethics and Professional Standards 60

10. Mediation and Customer Satisfaction in the Hospitality Industry 60

11. Mediation as a Preventive Measure for Disputes in the Hospitality Industry 62

12. Mediation Effects on Burnout and Turnover in Hotel Staff 63

13. Mediation and Vendor Relationships in the Hospitality Industry 64

14. Mediation and Guest Complaints in the Hospitality Industry 65

15. Mediation and Contractual Disputes in the Hospitality Industry 66

16. Mediation and Intellectual Property Issues in the Hospitality Industry 68

17. Mediation and Environmental Concerns in the Hospitality Industry 69

18. Mediation and Technology-Related Disputes in the Hospitality Industry 71

19. Mediation and Workplace Diversity in the Hospitality Industry 73

20. Mediation and International Disputes in the Hospitality Industry 75

A. Resolving Hotel Management Agreement Disputes 75

B. Disputes Over Contractual Obligations. 76

21. Mediation and Brand Reputation in the Hospitality Industry 77

22. Mediation and Financial Disputes in the Hospitality Industry 78

23. Mediation and Regulatory Compliance in the Hospitality Industry. 79

24. Mediation and Corporate Social Responsibility in the Hospitality Industry. 81

25. Comparison of Litigation and Mediation in the Hospitality Industry. 82

1. Introduction to Litigation and Mediation in the Hospitality Industry. 82

2. Litigation and Mediation in the Hospitality Industry. 82

3. Advantages of Mediation Over Litigation in the Hospitality Industry. 83

4. Conclusion. 84

CHAPTER SEVEN: TECHNIQUES FOR EFFECTIVE MEDIATION	86

1. . Optimizing Mediation Outcomes 86

1.1. Definition and Purpose. 86

1.2. Benefits and Limitations 87

2. . Key Principles of Mediation. 87

2.1. Neutrality and Impartiality 88

2.2. Confidentiality. 88

3. . Communication Skills for Mediators. 89

3.1. Active Listening. 90

3.2. Empathy and Emotional Intelligence 91

4. . Conflict Resolution Strategies 92

4.1. Interest-Based Bargaining 94

4.2. Brainstorming. 95

5. . Cultural Sensitivity in Mediation. 96

5.1. Understanding Cultural Differences 97

5.2. Avoiding Cultural Misunderstandings. 98

6. . Power Imbalance and Fairness 99

6.1. Addressing Power Dynamics 100

6.2 Ensuring Fairness. 102

6.3 Ethical Considerations in Mediation *103*

6.4 Conflict of Interest *104*

7 . Technology and Mediation 105

7.1. The rise of ODR *105*

7.2. Cybersecurity and Privacy Concerns *107*

CHAPTER EIGHT: IMPLEMENTATION OF MEDIATION POLICY AND PROCEDURE	109

1. . The Importance of Mediation Policy and Procedure 109

2. . Key Components of a Mediation Policy 109

A. Designing an Effective Mediation Procedure *109*

B. Training and Education for Mediators *113*

3. Legal Considerations in Mediation Policies 113

4. Measuring the Effectiveness of Mediation Policies 114

5. Confidentiality and Ethics 115

6. Conclusion and Future Trends 116

About the Author

Mohamed Darwish, renowned for his expertise in business development and legal acumen within the hospitality and real estate sectors. Mohamed's academic journey includes earning a PGDL (Postgraduate Diploma of Law) from Leeds Beckett University and pursuing a Master of Business Administration at the University of Leicester, UK. He also holds dual bachelor's degrees in business administration and law from the University of Cairo. As the founder of Darwish Legal Consultants in United Arab of Emirates (UAE), Mohamed specializes in providing tailored legal counsel and strategic support to esteemed hospitality organizations and companies across various jurisdictions in the UAE. With over 18 years of experience, Mohamed has held influential roles in the hospitality industry, spearheading strategic initiatives as the Head of Business Development in multiple organizations. He has successfully implemented comprehensive business plans, adding diverse hotels ranging from boutique to luxurious resorts across the Gulf Cooperation Countries (GCC), Turkey, and the Comoros Islands.

Moreover, Mohamed is a certified mediator accredited by the International Mediation Institute, showcasing his commitment to alternative dispute resolution. This certification, obtained through the ADR Center and supported by the legal department of the government in Dubai, underscores Mohamed's role as a trusted mediator in complex legal matters. In his debut book, "The Art of Mediation - The Key to Resolving Disputes in the Hospitality Industry," Mohamed shares insights into employing mediation as a more efficient alternative to lengthy litigation processes. Drawing from his extensive experience and innovative approach, Mohamed believes that mediation holds immense potential to streamline conflict resolution and foster positive outcomes in the hospitality sector. With his unique blend of business acumen, legal proficiency, and mediation skills, Mohamed is well-equipped to navigate multifaceted legal challenges, ensure compliance, and drive growth in dynamic industries.

Dedication

"I want to convey my deepest gratitude to God, whose constant guidance and support have been crucial throughout my journey. His blessings have persistently fuelled my determination to strive for excellence.

I am profoundly thankful to my mother, whose boundless love and incredible strength have shaped the person I am today. Her resilience and sacrifices have served as a continuous source of inspiration, pushing me forward through life's challenges.

My sincere appreciation also goes to my wife, who has been my anchor and pillar of support at every stage. Her unwavering belief in me, has been foundational to my success. Her encouragement and consistent support enabled me to pursue my dream of becoming a lawyer and obtaining my mediation certificate. I am eternally grateful for her love, guidance, and presence in my life.

Additionally, I dedicate this achievement as a tribute to my father, who passed away when I was young. Though I had only twelve years with him, his influence and legacy have profoundly shaped my life. His guidance and example laid the groundwork for my accomplishments today, and his memory continues to inspire me to strive for excellence and make a positive impact in everything I do.

Let's begin the
"Journey of Harmony"

CHAPTER ONE

INTRODUCTION TO THE HOSPITALITY INDUSTRY

*"Peace is not merely a distant goal that we seek, but
a means by which we arrive at that goal."*
Martin Luther King Jr

CHAPTER ONE: INTRODUCTION TO THE HOSPITALITY INDUSTRY

1. **The Evolution of Hospitality: From Ancient Times to Modern Era**

Hospitality, deeply ingrained in human history, has evolved significantly over ages. Ancient civilizations such as Mesopotamia, Egypt, and Greece esteemed hospitality as a sacred duty, where travellers were treated with reverence and generosity.

In Mesopotamia, hospitality was enshrined in the Code of Hammurabi, one of the earliest known legal codes. This code not only regulated various aspects of daily life but also emphasized the obligations of hosts towards travellers. It dictated fair treatment, provision of shelter, and even financial compensation for any harm suffered by guests. Hospitality wasn't merely a cultural norm but a legal and moral obligation, reflecting the fundamental values of Mesopotamian society.[1]

Similarly, ancient Egyptian texts provide rich insights into the importance of hospitality in society. Hospitality was viewed not only as a social duty but as a divine mandate. Guests were believed to be manifestations of gods, and hosting them was a way to honour the divine. The Egyptian concept of hospitality extended beyond mere material provisions; it encompassed rituals of purification, protection, and entertainment. Guests were treated with utmost respect and care, with hosts going to great lengths to ensure their comfort and well-being.[2]

Greek civilization further refined the concept of hospitality with the practice of "xenia." Xenia was more than just a set of rules; it was a sacred bond between guest and host, governed by mutual respect and reciprocity. The hospitality shown towards strangers was believed to reflect one's character and virtue. Violating xenia was not only a breach of social etiquette but a transgression against the gods, inviting divine punishment. Xenia played a central role in Greek mythology and literature, with stories illustrating the consequences of both exemplary and deficient hospitality.[3]

In ancient Rome, commercial hospitality establishments were categorized into four main types: hospitia, stabula, tabernae, and popinae. These establishments were used by travelers, merchants, and sailors for trade and selling, or overnight stops. They were not always standalone businesses but often connected to other establishments. The oldest collection of texts related to hospitality is found in the Near East, often read in parallel with the Old Testament. The Old Testament emphasizes hospitality and treating human life with respect and dignity, with laws requiring hospitality and concern for strangers. The New Testament also incorporates the concept of a messianic banquet, reflecting the redeemed humanity's hospitality. The Old Testament and New Testament both emphasize the importance of hospitality and respect for strangers.[4]

The Middle Ages witnessed a continuation of the hospitality traditions established in antiquity, albeit with distinct religious and cultural influences. Monasteries and religious orders became focal points of hospitality, offering shelter, sustenance, and spiritual guidance to pilgrims and travellers. Monastic hospitality was grounded in the Christian principle of charity and was seen as a way to fulfil Christ's commandment to "welcome the stranger." Monasteries provided refuge for the weary and vulnerable, embodying the ideals of compassion, humility, and service.[5]

Hospitality and generosity are core principles in Islamic culture, valued by the majority of Muslims, who

---

1 Van de Mieroop, M. (2005). King Hammurabi of Babylon: A Biography. John Wiley & Sons.(Caviris, A. X. (2011, April). King Hammurabi of Babylon: A Biography. By Marc van de Mieroop. Malden: Blackwell, 2005. Pp. xii + 171. $27.95 (paperback). *Journal of Near Eastern Studies*, 70(1), 127–129. https://doi.org/10.1086/659043

2 Assmann, J. (1996). The Mind of Egypt: History and Meaning in the Time of the Pharaohs. Harvard University Press. (Assmann, J. (2003, January 1). The Mind of Egypt. Harvard University)

3 D. Lenfant, "The role of xenia in diplomatic relations between Greek cities and the Persian Empire," in Good Faith. Modes of Communication in Ancient ..., 2022. [HTML].

4 D O'Gorman. (n.d.). Modern Hospitality: Lessons from the past August 2005. Journal of Hospitality and Tourism Management 12(2):131-141.

5 Vauchez, A. (1997). Sainthood in the Later Middle Ages. Cambridge University Press.

have a worldwide population of over 1.6 billion. Islamic hospitality involves giving voluntarily and without compensation, involving acts, words, and objects to honour guests and maintain good relationships. It is a culture that strengthens social relationships and unites individuals in integrated communities.

Hospitality is associated with core concepts of grace or blessing (baraka) and cosmic sustenance (al-rizq), represented in God's name al-Razzaq (meaning "the Sustainer" or "the Provider"). It enables people to become receptive to divine mercy and compassion. Muslims are concerned with the notion of social, economic, and divine cover (as-satr) as related to the scheme of the cosmological paradigm of sustenance or source of revenue, which belongs to the unseen world (qalam al-ghaib), dominated by God.

Islam is not a monolithic religion, with diverse Muslim communities. Islamic hospitality is influenced by social and historical factors and is multifaceted and diverse. It is associated with rites of passage, such as the birth of a child, marriage, and death. It is also an important aspect of Islamic religious holidays and rituals, such as the holy month of Ramadan, the Feast of Sacrifice, the Prophet's birthday, and the night journey and ascension of the Prophet.[6]

Throughout history, the hospitality industry emerged as a response to the practical need for lodging and sustenance during long journeys. Inns, taverns, and roadside shelters were established along trade routes and pilgrimage paths, offering weary travellers a place to rest, refresh, and recuperate. These establishments played a vital role in facilitating commerce, communication, and cultural exchange, contributing to the development of vibrant and interconnected societies.[7] The evolution of hospitality from ancient times to the modern era reflects not only changes in social norms and cultural practices but also shifts in economic structures, technological advancements, and geopolitical developments. While the forms and expressions of hospitality may have evolved over time, its underlying ethos of generosity, empathy, and human connection remains enduringly relevant in today's globalized world.

2. Disputes in the Ancient Hospitality Industry

I. *Disagreements and Conflicts in the Ancient Greek Society*

The Greek case is just one instance of the prevalence of hospitality in the ancient world, as seen in various religious, historical, and philosophical writings. Guest-related issues have also been addressed in laws throughout the Mediterranean region. It is fascinating to note that ancient Near Eastern laws spanning over 2000 years, from the first law code known as the Laws of Ur-Namma (issued during the Ur III period from 2112 to 2004 BCE) to the Justinian Code (issued by Byzantine Justinian in 534), regulated the protection of foreign travellers within the state. Despite being a fundamental concept that has been practiced for centuries, the intricacies of this "right of reception" are not fully grasped by contemporary scholars.

The earliest legal dispute in history can be traced back to The Odyssey, a well-known epic poem written by Homer. This literary work sparked deep contemplation in ancient Greek society during a time when hospitality was highly valued and seen as a virtue. Unlike today where luxurious hotels cater to guests, it was the duty of virtuous and religious individuals to warmly welcome and extend kind hospitality to strangers. This raised a complex question for the Greeks: should virtuous hosts be obliged to embrace and entertain transient wanderers, or should it fall upon the duty of town rulers to offer their goodwill-driven hospitality? These weighty concerns troubled Greek society as they searched for a definitive answer in the midst of unfortunate events. It was during this tumultuous period that Achilles, the legendary warrior, emerged as a guiding light, shedding light on the uncertain path ingrained in Greek tradition. Eighty years have since

---

[6] el-Sayed el-Aswad. "Hospitality (in Islam)." ENCYCLOPEDIA OF ISLAM AND THE MUSLIM WORLD, Cengage Learning Inc, Farmington Hills, MI (2015): n. pag. Print.

[7] Pine, B. J., & Gilmore, J. H. (1999). The Experience Economy: Work Is Theatre & Every Business a Stage. Harvard Business Press.

passed since the Iliad, yet conflicts among different social groups are still depicted. Fearlessly, Achilles addressed these perplexing issues and emphasized the importance of cherishing and safeguarding visitors from foreign lands. His unwavering support for providing shelter and protection to the lost individuals left an indelible mark on ancient Greece that continues to resonate even today. In the tumult captured within the Iliad, Achilles fearlessly brought clarity to these bewildering inquiries, emphasizing the utmost importance of cherishing and safeguarding foreign travellers. His passionate advocacy for harboring and protecting those who were lost left a deep impression on ancient Greece, surpassing the test of time.

II. *Roman Empire Drama: Ancient Times' Turmoil.*

It is commonly known that in Roman law, lesser obligations were derived from wedding contracts and patron-client relationships, with additional obligations that could be mutually agreed upon by the parties involved. However, it is worth noting that the explicit mention of less binding hospitality-games cannot be found in the legal literature of Roman or Byzantine law. The focus of these legal texts primarily revolves around practical accusations and defences rather than abstract legal discussions. Nonetheless, within the Digest, there are two interesting mentions that vaguely refer to acts of kindness, which, if frequently practiced within the same household, could potentially develop into contractual obligations. From my understanding, these mentions encompass not only acts related to hospitality itself but also a wider range of friendly gestures, such as exchanging gifts or hosting light-hearted banquets. As a playful analogy, this could include not only offering a bottle of wine but also engaging in small pranks, like jokingly throwing a coat hanger across the room to induce amusement

If a host made a promise to entertain a guest and failed to fulfil the offered hospitality, according to the legal literature, the guest could have taken legal action for breach of contract. However, in reality, it would have been difficult for a guest to present their case and win the lawsuit. One might even speculate that Roman law might have discouraged guests from bringing their hosts to court. Theoretically, a guest who had been invited by a host could have refused to leave or declined the invitation altogether, claiming a reasonable fear of their host's disloyalty. In fact, such rejections of hospitality can be found in esteemed classical literature. Horace, for example, mentions that many invitees vote against attending a dinner gathering.

During ancient Rome, there existed a legal provision where a guest had the right to legally challenge a host who failed to honour their commitment to provide hospitality. Historical records from that time attest to the existence of legal literature regarding this matter. However, it is crucial to acknowledge that guests faced numerous challenges in seeking redress and winning their lawsuits. Some might even argue that the Roman legal system incorporated certain deterrents to discourage guests from pursuing legal action against their hosts. Moreover, in theory, a guest who received an invitation from a host had the choice to decline, based on a genuine concern about the host's lack of loyalty. Examples of such rejections, motivated by a well-founded fear of the host's unreliability, can be found in esteemed classical literature. In fact, the esteemed poet Horace recounts that a significant number of individuals intentionally declined invitations to dine due to similar concerns.

3. **The Rise of Hospitality as a Lucrative Industry**

The 19th century marked a pivotal period in the transformation of hospitality from a customary practice to a thriving industry. This transition was fueled by several key factors, including advancements in transportation, urbanization, and industrialization.

The Industrial Revolution, which began in the late 18th century and continued into the 19th century, brought about significant changes in society, economy, and technology. One of the most notable impacts was the revolutionization of transportation. The introduction of steamships and railways revolutionized travel, making long-distance journeys faster, safer, and more affordable than ever before. This accessibility paved the way for the growth of tourism and spurred the development of hospitality infrastructure to accommodate the influx of travellers.

Urbanization also played a crucial role in the rise of the hospitality industry. As people flocked to cities in search of employment opportunities and better lives, urban centres became bustling hubs of activity and commerce. Hotels, restaurants, and entertainment venues sprang up to cater to the needs and desires of urban dwellers and visiting travellers. The concentration of population and economic activity in cities created a fertile ground for the expansion of hospitality services and establishments.

The 19th century witnessed the emergence of grand hotels that epitomized the era of luxury and opulence. Iconic establishments like the Ritz in Paris and the Waldorf Astoria in New York set new standards of excellence in hospitality, offering unparalleled comfort, service, and sophistication to their discerning clientele. These grand hotels became symbols of prestige and glamour, attracting wealthy travellers, dignitaries, and celebrities from around the world.

The World's Columbian Exposition, held in Chicago in 1893, served as a landmark event that showcased the potential of hospitality as an economic force. The exposition, commemorating the 400th anniversary of Christopher Columbus's arrival in the Americas, attracted millions of visitors from across the globe. The sheer scale and success of the event demonstrated the capacity of hospitality to drive tourism, stimulate economic growth, and showcase the cultural and technological achievements of nations[8].

Overall, the 19th century marked a period of unprecedented growth and transformation for the hospitality industry. Advancements in transportation, urbanization, and industrialization fueled the expansion of hospitality services and infrastructure, while iconic establishments and landmark events helped elevate the industry's profile and significance on the global stage.[9][10][11]

---

8   Britannica, T. Editors of Encyclopaedia. "World's Columbian Exposition." *Encyclopedia Britannica*, February 2, 2024. https://www.britannica.com/event/Worlds-Columbian-Exposition.
9   D. Lambert and P. Merriman, "Empire and mobility: an introduction," in Mobility in the Long Nineteenth Century, 2020, manchesterhive.com. amazonaws.com
10 T. Ewertowski, "Bodies in networks: steamship mobilities and travel between Europe and Asia, 1869–1891," Mobilities, 2024.
11 J. Bailey and J. Bailey, "… in Forms of Transport—Steam Locomotives, Cycle Tyres, Oceanic Liners, and Jet Aircraft. Transport Infrastructure—Canals, Roads, and Commercial Railways," in … British Scientists and Engineers and Five Centuries of …, Springer, 2022.

CHAPTER TWO

CHALLENGES IN THE HOSPITALITY INDUSTRY

"Peace is not the absence of conflict, but the ability to cope with it." — Mahatma Gandhi

CHAPTER TWO: CHALLENGES IN THE HOSPITALITY INDUSTRY

1. Complexity of Operations: Guest Needs Across Departments

The hotel sector has evolved from the nineteenth century to the present, and it now operates in a dynamic environment loaded with obstacles and complications. From managing guest expectations to navigating technological developments, hospitality professionals must be able to adapt to a wide range of issues to maintain their operations' success and sustainability.

Consider this scenario: a guest checks into a hotel and asks a late checkout. This seemingly simple request necessitates collaboration among the front office, housekeeping, and reservations staff. The front office must guarantee that the guest's request is noted and conveyed to the housekeeping so that their cleaning schedule can be adjusted accordingly. Meanwhile, the reservation department must update their system to reflect the extended stay, to ensure the room is not assigned to another guest.

Another example is when a guest reserves a hotel for a special event, such as a honeymoon or anniversary. This guest may have special preferences, such as a room with a view, a bottle of champagne upon arrival, or rose petals on the bed. Fulfilling these demands requires teamwork among several departments, including reservations, housekeeping, and food and beverage, to ensure that the guest's experience exceeds expectations.

In the sales and marketing department, employees may compete to secure corporate accounts or group bookings. This competition can sometimes lead to conflicts when multiple sales representatives target the same client or when promises made by one representative conflict with the offerings of another. For example, if two sales representatives independently offer discounted rates to the same corporate client, it can create confusion and potentially damage the hotel's reputation.

Similarly, conflicts may arise between the front office and reservation departments when handling room assignments and guest requests. For instance, if a guest requests a room with a king-size bed but is assigned a room with two twin beds due to a miscommunication between departments, it can result in dissatisfaction and complaints.

Consider a scenario where a hotel hosts a wedding reception in its banquet hall. The events department works closely with the bride and groom to plan the details of the event, including seating arrangements, menu selections, and decor. However, if the food and beverage department receive last-minute requests for dietary restrictions or changes to the menu, it can create challenges in coordinating with the events team to ensure a seamless experience for the guests.

Additionally, conflicts may arise between the sales department and other departments when negotiating contracts for events or group bookings. For example, if the sales department promises exclusive use of a certain space or amenities to a client without consulting with the operations or food and beverage teams, it can lead to overcommitment and operational challenges.

In summary, these examples highlight the intricate nature of operations within the hospitality industry and the importance of effective communication and collaboration between departments to ensure guest satisfaction and mitigate potential conflicts.

2. Transition from Transactional to Relationship Marketing

In recent years, the hospitality industry has witnessed a paradigm shift from transactional to relationship marketing. Traditionally, hotels and resorts focused on driving immediate bookings and maximizing revenue through promotional offers and discounts. However, in today's hyperconnected world, building long-term relationships with guests has become paramount.

Relationship marketing emphasizes the importance of cultivating meaningful connections with guests throughout their journey, from initial inquiry to post-stay engagement. This entails personalized communication, anticipatory service, and loyalty programs tailored to individual preferences and behaviours. By nurturing these relationships, hospitality establishments can foster guest loyalty, generate repeat business, and drive positive word-of-mouth referrals.

However, implementing effective relationship marketing strategies face challenges in the digital age. With consumers bombarded by promotional content across various digital platforms, standing out and forming genuine connections can be challenging. Moreover, maintaining consistency and relevance across various touchpoints—from social media and email marketing to face-to-face interactions—requires strategic planning and meticulous execution.

In many cases, the designated departments tasked with managing guest feedback and disputes lack the necessary resources and expertise to handle these issues effectively, particularly when it comes to online feedback. For instance, imagine a situation where a guest posts a negative review about their experience on a hotel's social media page. Frontline employees, who may not be well-versed in online complaint management, might resort to using templated responses copied from other sources. However, this approach can sometimes exacerbate the situation, as guests may perceive the responses as impersonal and insincere. Without proper training and guidance on handling online complaints, frontline staff may struggle to address guests' concerns in a manner that resonates positively with them, potentially leading to further dissatisfaction and negative word-of-mouth.

Let's reimagine the scenario in an online context, where the General Manager (GM) of a hotel holds significant authority over the hotel's operations, and the management company, which owns the hotel brand, is not heavily involved in day-to-day affairs.

Picture this: a guest books a room through the hotel's website but encounters issues upon check-in, such as a discrepancy in room type or amenities. Frustrated, the guest reaches out to the hotel's customer service via email or social media, seeking resolution for the problem. The frontline staff, lacking specialized training in handling online complaints, may respond using templated responses copied from other sources, inadvertently worsening the situation.

Now, the guest, dissatisfied with the initial response, escalates the matter to the GM, expecting a swift and satisfactory resolution. However, despite the GM's operational expertise, they may lack the specialized knowledge required to effectively address online guest disputes. In an attempt to resolve the issue swiftly, the GM might offer a discount or complimentary stay without fully understanding the root cause of the problem or considering the hotel's policies.

While this immediate resolution might pacify the guest momentarily, it could establish a precedent for similar disputes in the future and lead to inconsistencies in handling similar cases. Moreover, the GM's decision may not align with the hotel's broader goals, or the policies set by the management company.

Without proper training or guidelines on online guest dispute resolution, the GM's actions could result in unresolved conflicts, negative online reviews, or even legal ramifications. Ultimately, this could tarnish the hotel's reputation and impact its profitability.

In this scenario, the hierarchical structure within the hotel, coupled with the lack of specialized training in online dispute resolution, may inadvertently contribute to ineffective handling of guest complaints and inconsistent outcomes.

To address these challenges, hotel operators must consider alternative approaches to handling disputes. This may involve appointing individuals with specialized training and authority, separate from hotel management, to oversee guest relations and dispute resolution. These individuals would possess the necessary knowledge and authority, gained from the operator's head office, to address disputes promptly and effectively, thereby minimizing the risk of guest dissatisfaction and disputes.

3. Impact of Social Media and Digital Platforms: The Double-Edged Sword

The way that customers engage with and see hospitality businesses has completely changed as a result of the emergence of social media and digital platforms. Social media sites such as Facebook, Instagram, and TripAdvisor have become essential resources for hotels and resorts to promote their properties. For instance, hotels can interact directly with clients on Facebook to respond to questions and provide real-time feedback, or they can share gorgeous images of their rooms on Instagram to draw in new visitors.

But these opportunities also bring with them difficulties. Hotels are increasingly exposed to public scrutiny and criticism as content generation has become more democratic. A hotel's reputation might suffer greatly from unfavourable ratings on websites like Yelp or TripAdvisor. Imagine a visitor to a hotel leaving a critical TripAdvisor review describing their unsatisfactory encounter with poor standards of cleanliness and service. The hotel's credibility may be harmed by this review, which may discourage prospective visitors from making reservations.

Moreover, the influence of visitor comments is enhanced by social media's real-time nature. Social media users are quick to share complaints from other guests about noisy rooms or delayed room service, which can quickly go viral and harm the hotel's reputation. If a visitor tweets, for example, about how delayed the hotel is responding to their request for room service, it might become viral and change people's opinions about the quality of the hotel's services.

To effectively handle these issues, restaurants and hotels need to approach social media management with a proactive and strategic mindset. Hotels must keep a close eye on internet discussions and react quickly to both positive and negative feedback from their guests. For instance, the hotel may send out a thank-you tweet and extend an invitation to return if a visitor tweets about how much they enjoyed their meal at the restaurant. Through genuine engagement on social media, hotels can cultivate brand loyalty and establish authentic relationships with their customers.

In summary, the hospitality sector faces a wide range of difficulties, from evolving marketing tactics to operational complexity and digital disruption. However, hospitality organizations may not only adapt to this constantly changing environment, but also prosper in it by embracing change, utilizing technology to its full potential, and prioritizing client happiness even more.

CHAPTER THREE

LITIGATION IN THE HOSPITALITY INDUSTRY

"Peace cannot be achieved through violence, it can only be attained through understanding." — Ralph Waldo Emerson

CHAPTER THREE: LITIGATION IN THE HOSPITALITY INDUSTRY

1. The Rise of Complaints and Disputes: Hotel, Guest, and the Travel Agent.

Since the evolution of the digital era from transactional marketing, disputes also evolved in the hospitality industry. In the past, you might find that there was no way of two-way communication. Usually, the travel agent who booked the guest from their home to the hotel was the only way to communicate. If there was any complaint from the guest, the guest complained to the travel agent, who subsequently complained to the hotel. Then the hotel provided their feedback, and consequently, the guest received it. This line of communication made it difficult to determine conflicts. Sometimes, due to the strong connection between the hotel and the travel agent, the guest could get lost in the communication. Somehow, the travel agents used to calm down the guest, as there was no need to escalate things, simply because the travel agent did not want to lose their reputation or their connection with the hotel, and they also tried hard to find an amicable solution with the guest to avoid cancellations or the guest not using the same travel agent again.

Some may think that the travel agent here could act as a mediator. Simply put, this was not mediation but frustration since the guest was not able to assert their rights, the hotel provided minimal to no solution, and the travel agent had nothing to do except remain silent. Some travel agencies who were expert in dealing with hotels knew exactly the problems associated with the hotels and tried to avoid these kinds of issues happening with their guests. For example, the travel agent might ask the front office manager or the reservation agent during the reservation to block rooms facing the other side of the hotel to avoid construction noise, or they might ask them to block rooms where the air conditioner was working well. These considerations might apply to guests who paid a lot for their visit, while others who paid less just to enjoy the city did not have problems with such issues. The travel agent could not be in a mediator position here because they favoured solutions that worked best for them more than their guest.

Over time, when guests started to book their rooms directly from online travel agencies (OTAs) such as Booking.com and Expedia.com, digital disputes evolved. Guests could now discover hotels with a fresh eye, sensing the difference and understanding that the amount they used to pay was not worth it anymore. Often, they left feedback that could lead to a decrease in bookings. This type of feedback made operators and owners more open to renovating the hotel to regain lost guests or attract more guests at higher rates. The game between the operator, the hotel owner, and the guest became clear: to get more bookings, the hotel needed to improve, receive more positive feedback, and justify higher prices by renovating. This loop will never end, and the digital era has made this process quicker with swift responses to avoid further complaints or disputes.

2. The Rise of Complaints and Disputes: Hotels and Employees

From the previous examples, we see that a hotel relies on a diverse team of personnel dedicated to meeting guests' needs and ensuring their stay is as comfortable as possible. However, these employees are influenced by various internal and external factors that can affect their moods and interactions with each other. Take, for instance, a guest booking scenario: Sarah booked a room through the hotel website (HWS), and the booking was confirmed. She took the initiative to call the hotel to request special amenities for her anniversary, planning to surprise her husband. Despite her efforts, no one initially answered her calls. After several attempts, she finally reached someone. "Hello, good afternoon, this is Mike, how may I assist you?" he said. Frustrated by the lack of response, Sarah started yelling and shouting. Instead of calmly handling her complaint, Mike, equally frustrated, responded harshly. This led Sarah to cancel her booking and post a scathing review on social media, warning other travellers to avoid the hotel due to her negative experience before even arriving.

Let's examine the employee's perspective. Mike was left alone on the afternoon shift with no support, as management assumed that the hotel was busier in the morning and quieter from the afternoon till night. They concentrated their team in the morning and minimized staffing in the afternoon to avoid complaints. However, this decision backfired. Mike was overwhelmed, juggling multiple calls while dealing with Sarah's escalating frustration. On top of this, he was preoccupied with personal stress, such as his car's major engine problem that he could only repair after his salary was paid. The management, failing to consider these factors, decided to fire Mike due to the increased complaints during his shift.

Feeling unjustly treated, Mike chose not to file a complaint with HR, knowing the strong connection between HR and management would likely result in his case being ignored. Instead, he filed a police report, detailing the psychological distress caused by being assigned to the afternoon shift for six months. This schedule prevented him from attending to personal matters and spending time with his family, and constantly dealing with guest complaints took a toll on his mental health. Mike's report highlighted how hearing requests like Sarah's for special anniversary amenities affected him emotionally.

Now there is a dispute involving the hotel general manager (GM), Mike, and HR. This conflict, stemming from a poor management decision, has put the hotel in a crisis. Either Mike or the GM will prevail, and it's clear who has the upper hand. Such scenarios are common across service industries, including restaurants and cafes. However, the hospitality industry, with its high number of daily interactions between diverse personnel and guests, is particularly prone to these conflicts.

This example underscores the daily disputes that arise in the hospitality sector, leading to various internal and external conflicts. These disputes often escalate to litigation, contributing to an overwhelming number of cases in courts. It's crucial to take a closer look at these disputes within the hospitality industry to understand their origins and impacts.

3. The Rise of Disputes and Legal Cases

Litigation in the hospitality industry includes a wide range of legal disputes, including those involving discrimination, contract breaches, antitrust violations, intellectual property disputes, consumer protection claims, employment law issues, and environmental regulations, among others. These legal fights provide significant difficulties and obstacles for both plaintiffs and defendants in the sector. A closer look at numerous in-depth case studies sheds light on the complexities of these conflicts and provide more understanding of the hospitality industry environment, whereas the complications that it faces on daily basis is not like any other industry else, let's see some of these ones:

Best Western International, Inc. v. James Furber, et al. was a complicated litigation against anonymous people who posted defamatory statements online that hurt the company's reputation. The court carefully analysed the plaintiff's claims and determined that they did not fulfill the criteria for an abuse of process claim. In their quest of justice, Best Western International, Inc. learned that the defamers were members of their own organization. Consequently, the court rejected the breach of contract claim since the membership contract did not contain a secrecy clause.

It is important to note that the court impartially examined the statements made by the defendants, assessing whether they were defamatory. Some statements were found to lack defamatory intent and were therefore not subject to legal consequences. Additionally, the court recognized that certain statements were protected by the concept of common interest privilege. Furthermore, the court's comprehensive analysis addressed not only the allegations of defamation but also matters related to interference with contractual relations and the calculation of appropriate damages. This highlights the intricate nature of legal disputes involving defamation, breach of contract, and unfair competition in the digital landscape.

Overall, this landmark case demonstrates the complexity and intricacy involved in legal disputes concerning defamation, breach of contract, and unfair competition in the digital sphere.

In Kenneth Munson v. Del Taco Inc., 522 F.3d 997 (9th Cir. 4/14/08). The plaintiff, who uses a wheelchair, was unable to enter the parking lot and amenities of a Del Taco restaurant in California owing to architectural barriers. He filed a lawsuit against, Karen Morris, Esq., Diana S. Barber, J.D., CHE, and James O. Eiler, Esq., alleging violations of the California Unruh Act and the Americans with Disabilities Act. The district court granted plaintiff partial summary judgment, ruling that there was no question of fact about the presence of an architectural barrier and that enlarging the toilet doorway was a feasible endeavour.

The conclusion of these cases, Alice Camarillo v. Carrols Corp., Magliocca Stores, et al. and Kenneth Munson v. Del Taco Inc., reinforces the significance of adhering to Americans with Disabilities Act (ADA) guidelines within the hospitality industry. These cases serve as a reminder that businesses have a legal responsibility to guarantee accessibility for people with disabilities. Failure to comply with ADA regulations can lead to severe consequences, such as expensive legal battles and harm to a company's reputation. Therefore, it is crucial for businesses in the hospitality sector to prioritize ADA compliance and take proactive measures to ensure equal access for all individuals. Neglecting these obligations may result in detrimental outcomes for both the company and the disabled community.

Furthermore, it is crucial to elaborate on the significance of contract disputes, as evidenced by Jamie Liebrand v. Brinker Restaurant Corporation and David W. Rutter v. Darden Restaurants Inc., et al., in order to fully understand the consequences and moral implications involved. These cases clearly illustrate the repercussions that arise when contractual agreements are not clear and enforceable in the hospitality industry. In Jamie Liebrand v. Brinker Restaurant Corporation and David W. Rutter v. Darden Restaurants Inc., et al., the courts' decisions shed light on the far-reaching effects of unclear contractual agreements. These disputes demonstrate the potential legal risks faced by hospitality businesses when agreements are not adequately drafted and enforced.

One of the key consequences highlighted by these cases is the need for procedural fairness. Without clear and enforceable contractual agreements, conflicts can escalate, leading to prolonged and costly legal battles. The absence of procedural guidelines can create confusion and uncertainty, making it difficult to reach a resolution efficiently.

As in David W. Rutter v. Darden Restaurants Inc., et al., 2008 WL 4949043 (C.D.Cal. 11/18/08). Plaintiff was employed at Red Lobster restaurants. In a booklet, the company had outlined a dispute resolution process that required employees to waive all rights to bring a civil court action in favor of mediation or, for state and federal claims, arbitration. Plaintiff argued that arbitration was optional, and the court disagreed finding that the language was clear that arbitration was mandatory. The court dismissed Plaintiff's claims without prejudice. The decision contains a good discussion about both procedural and substantive unconscionability vis-à-vis arbitration clauses.

The enforceability of arbitration agreements also plays a significant role in the outcome of contract disputes. These cases emphasize the importance of having well-documented arbitration clauses to resolve conflicts in a timely and cost-effective manner. The courts' decisions underline the effectiveness of arbitration as an alternative dispute resolution mechanism and its ability to mitigate legal risks for hospitality businesses.

In conclusion, after checking those cases[12], you find that the hospitality industry experiences various types of disputes that the courts are busy resolving, many of which could be settled amicably. For instance, Best Western and Del Taco restaurants have clear cases that we obtained from a legal channel to illustrate to

---

12 K. Morris, D. S. Barber, and J. O. Eiler, "Hospitality Case Review: The Top 100+ Cases That Impacted Us This Past Year," in Proceedings of the Seventh Annual Hospitality Law Conference, Feb. 9-11, 2009, Houston, TX.

the reader. If these disputes had been resolved amicably, I believe the names Best Western and Del Taco would not be known as either plaintiffs or defendants. Now, everyone is aware of these cases, and in the future, others may highlight them in different contexts. These cases have become examples that everyone must consider before attempting similar actions in the future. By learning from these examples, hospitality businesses can safeguard their interests and maintain a positive industry reputation, by learning from these examples, hospitality businesses can safeguard their interests and maintain a positive industry reputation.

4. Lengthy Procedures and Associated Costs

Litigation in the courts can be a time-consuming and expensive process for all parties involved. The adversarial nature of litigation, combined with complex legal frameworks and procedural requirements, often leads to lengthy legal battles that drain both time and resources. From the moment of filing to the comprehensive discovery processes, parties find themselves tangled in a complex system that exceeds their expectations. The trial proceedings, which can last for months or even years, become a difficult journey. Throughout this prolonged litigation process, parties involved in the litigation struggle to navigate through the intricate legal details, hoping for a favourable outcome. However, their hopes are burdened by the increasing strain on their finances and resources as they grapple with the weight of the system they are in.

In addition, it is crucial to acknowledge that the unknown and unpredictable nature of legal disputes can lead to significant challenges for hospitality establishments. These challenges directly affect their capability to operate effectively and make well-informed, strategic decisions. The mere possibility of enduring lengthy court processes and being faced with uncertain outcomes can greatly discourage businesses from pursuing litigation. Instead, they may be compelled to seek alternative methods of conflict resolution that enable swift resolution while also minimizing expenses. These complexities emphasize the need for a comprehensive understanding of the legal landscape within the hospitality industry, as well as the importance of implementing proactive measures to prevent and efficiently manage potential legal disputes. By doing so, hospitality establishments can navigate the potential obstacles and uncertainties associated with legal complexities, ensuring their ability to operate efficiently and implement effective decision-making strategies.

The ramifications of litigation on the hospitality industry are crucial to examine. In an ever-evolving legal landscape, it's important to consider whether litigation will persist in the coming years. With the rise of Artificial Intelligence (AI) and its impact on our fast-paced world, it becomes even more crucial for hospitality leaders to take proactive measures to mitigate risks and promptly resolve issues. As the legal environment undergoes constant transformation, leaders in the hospitality sector must navigate with vigilance to protect the well-being and effectiveness of their establishments. Additionally, it's essential for leaders in the hospitality industry to learn from legal cases such as those involving Best Western and Del Taco restaurants and understand their legal implications. While these cases set precedents in the legal court system, some in the hospitality industry are ignored or not given due consideration. Some management teams understand that each hotel has its distinctive nature, and not every case can be treated the same. Unfortunately, from my experience, cases like those involving Del Taco and Best Western are encountered frequently, albeit with different people and hotel names. Some plaintiffs, such as those in the Del Taco case, may not need to resort to courts if they can find a solution independently or communicate directly with management. However, there have been instances where management has responded with unfair or irrelevant comments, such as " We are sorry but this is the structure of the hotel, can we offer an orange juice as a complimentary?" Some others would say " our apologies of the inconvenience, we will consider this in the future". These statements can be frustrating for visitors and guests as they fail to provide a satisfactory solution. Management often relies on these "templates" in challenging situations, without considering their impact on guests, especially in an era where AI may play a significant role in legal implications. Some guests may opt to bring their case to an AI Assistant specialized in the hospitality industry assigned from the government to resolve things amicably according to the implemented legislations and other solutions provided by legal, arbitrators and mediators experts in the field, which could potentially reshape their response to the manager.

"My apologies, but the offer of orange juice won't quite solve the problem at hand. I've raised my concerns with the Amicable Conflict Resolution (ACR) app, and they're dispatching our AI Robot, "Serene", to check out the facility and provide an immediate solution. Here's hoping your orange juice serves as a helpful boost for Serene's battery! You see, if Serene finds an issue, the resolution protocol kicks in. It's either a full compensation for my stay, plus a promise of a complimentary future stay if the issue isn't too severe, or a request for facility adjustments within 14 days, along with that future stay. Funny thing, I didn't even try your orange juice yet; who knows, it might have been another case to address!"[13]

5. The Need for Alternative Dispute Resolution (ADR)

Since that we have experienced some development in the digital era that involved AI in our daily routine and given the drawbacks of traditional litigation, there is a growing recognition of the need for ADR mechanisms within the hospitality sector. ADR methods, such as mediation and arbitration, offer parties a more expedient and cost-effective means of resolving disputes while preserving business relationships and reputations.

In addition to the legal cases previously mentioned, in the gulf region and particularly in the United Arab of Emirates (UAE), the right of litigants to seek justice is protected under Article 6 of the UAE Constitution and Articles 94, 100, and 101 of the Federal Judiciary Law. ADR procedures were added to the legal system by the UAE to encourage a flexible approach to dispute resolution considering the growing demand for speedy and affordable legal processes. In the aftermath of the pandemic, the significance of ADR has been emphasized even more. To guarantee the uninterrupted administration of justice and to make it easier for litigants to access the legal system, ADR could be repurposed to incorporate internet technology, digitization, and virtual hearings. The judicial system may only be strengthened more through the extension and use of ADR procedures during and after the Covid-19 outbreak, by guaranteeing that, litigants are provided with effective dispute resolution mechanisms. While preserving core values, this has accelerated ADR's transformation in the UAE into a reputable, dynamic, and adaptive process while upholding basic values.

Regarding the ADR processes, the UAE has also taken significant measures to ensure that justice is played a convenient role and can be practiced at ease. A new federal law that unifies the several statutes on conciliation and mediation in civil and business disputes under a unified legal framework was released by the United Arab Emirates on September 28, 2023. The goal of the law, which went into effect on December 29, 2023, is to simplify the procedures and processes for settling disagreements peacefully, whether they arise before or during court proceedings.

In order to promote the resolution of conflicts through the involvement of a neutral third party, the law calls for the creation of online platforms or mediation and conciliation centres within the first-instance courts. The law permits the establishment of branches of foreign mediation centres, as well as independent mediation centres, in the UAE, one of the newly established non-profit organization (The Mediation Hub MENA) is a DIFC-based non-profit organization, its mission includes creating a network for mediators and advancing a culture of mediation in the MENA region. of which I am proud to be a member. The hub was founded by Christine Maksoud, a Lebanese qualified lawyer and solicitor of England & Wales, who has been practicing in the UAE since 2016. She holds a senior position at Al Tamimi & Company.

---
13 This example is for demonstration purposes only and does not have any connection with reality in any way, especially not at the present time.

As Dubai's hotel industry has become a thriving and dynamic sector on a global scale. Once primarily known for its luxurious offerings, it has now expanded its range to appeal to a wider range of visitors, showcasing its maturity. In addition to the well-established five-star hotels, there has been a noticeable increase in mid-range and family-friendly accommodations to meet the growing demands of visitors who are attracted to the city's theme parks and different entertainment growing facilities.

The $1.2 billion 'Viceroy' Palm Jumeirah Hotel struggle is only one example of how previous press reports have shown the seriousness of conflicts within the business that need to be addressed and resolved through another system or mechanism to ensure the smooth operation of the sector. The owner of the property, FIVE Holdings, and the previous operator, Viceroy Hotels and Resorts, got into an argument. Their arguments turned into a legal battle involving both offshore and onshore courts, with accusations of forcible removals and abrupt management shifts.[14]

This case emphasizes the importance of alternative methods for resolving disputes, such as mediation. While some aspects of the conflict may require private arbitration, mediation offers a collaborative platform to address underlying grievances and seek mutually beneficial solutions. As the industry potentially undergoes shifts in its operational dynamics, mediation could prove to be a crucial tool in navigating conflicts and fostering sustainable relationships between hotel owners and operators.

Moreover, ADR mechanisms offer parties greater flexibility and confidentiality in addressing sensitive issues, fostering collaborative problem-solving and mutually beneficial outcomes. By embracing ADR, hospitality businesses can enhance their dispute resolution strategies, minimize litigation costs, and maintain focus on their core operations and customer service.

In conclusion, litigation in the hospitality sector presents unique challenges and complexities for businesses, necessitating a strategic approach to dispute resolution. By examining case studies, understanding the associated costs and procedural hurdles, and embracing ADR mechanisms, hospitality businesses can effectively navigate legal challenges and safeguard their interests in an increasingly litigious environment.

---

14 A. Mcauley, "Fresh legal blows traded in Viceroy Palm hotel dispute," The National, Jul. 02, 2017. [Online]. Available: https://www.thenationalnews.com/business/fresh-legal-blows-traded-in-viceroy-palm-hotel-dispute-1.531010. [Accessed: May 06, 2024].

CHAPTER FOUR

THE ROLE OF ALTERNATIVE DISPUTE RESOLUTION IN THE HOSPITALITY INDUSTRY

"Let us put an end to wars, let us reshape life on the solid basis of equity and truth." - Anwar El Sadaat (The Former Egyptian President)

CHAPTER FOUR: THE ROLE OF ADR IN THE HOSPITALITY INDUSTRY

In this chapter, we will delve into the history, concept, and different types of ADR. We will also explore the two main models for ADR adoption by nations: the mandatory model and the voluntary model.

We will examine the strengths and weaknesses of ADR, both in a general sense and specifically within the dynamic hospitality industry. Furthermore, we will review the legislative frameworks implemented across different countries and regions to regulate the use of ADR within the industry. In addition, we will explore the innovative realm of online dispute resolution (ODR) and its profound implications for the hospitality sector. We will also investigate the application of ADR in resolving workplace disputes within the industry.

To conclude, this chapter will offer strategic recommendations aimed at enhancing the use of ADR in resolving disputes within the ever-evolving hospitality industry. We will also provide a roadmap for future research endeavours in this promising area, ensuring continual growth and refinement of ADR practices.

Traditionally, when discussing the concept of dispute resolution, the immediate thought involves using the court system to resolve the dispute. As a result of skyrocketing costs and the time and emotional energy consumed in utilizing the court system, more and more parties are turning to other mechanisms to resolve their disputes. ADR reduces the amount of time it takes to get a dispute resolved, lessens the burdens placed on the court system, and ultimately results in lower cost. This is particularly useful in relationships occurring within the hospitality industry, which itself is often built on relationships and guest satisfaction. Thus, ADR has gained significantly increased interest due to the benefits of speed, economic and interpersonal savings inherent in the settlement of disputes.

1. The Impact of Digital Age on Customer Feedback

The hospitality sector is prepared to manage the increasing trend of client testimonials on social media platforms. Word-of-mouth spreads online, giving customers—past and present—access to and a platform to discuss their interactions with a business. The visual, interactive, and networked aspects of social media enable managers to promptly pinpoint issues inside their organization and exchange input among team members to formulate remedial measures. Simple observations to unforeseen events like a building catching fire or discovering a leakage in the air conditioner in one of the guest rooms where they complained about, and it was going to affect the whole electrical system. The unpredictable nature of the topics that could be discussed on these online comments is illustrated by these stories. The hospitality sector is aware of how critical it is to monitor client feedback and respond to their concerns in a timely and effective manner.as it is often said: "Your reputation depends on the quality of your most recent hotel room or meal." Unlike traditional comment cards, such as the one shown in (Figure 1), Sometimes, Guest Comment Cards (GCC) are limited to specific questions, and at other times, only an open-ended question is provided. These types of cards do not capture the entire guest experience for elaboration. Additionally, they only facilitate one-way communication, with no expectation of replies from the management. Furthermore, these cards are either taken seriously and presented to the management during daily morning briefings or sometimes ignored, merely serving as formalities of the hotel operator or management's policy and procedures manual.

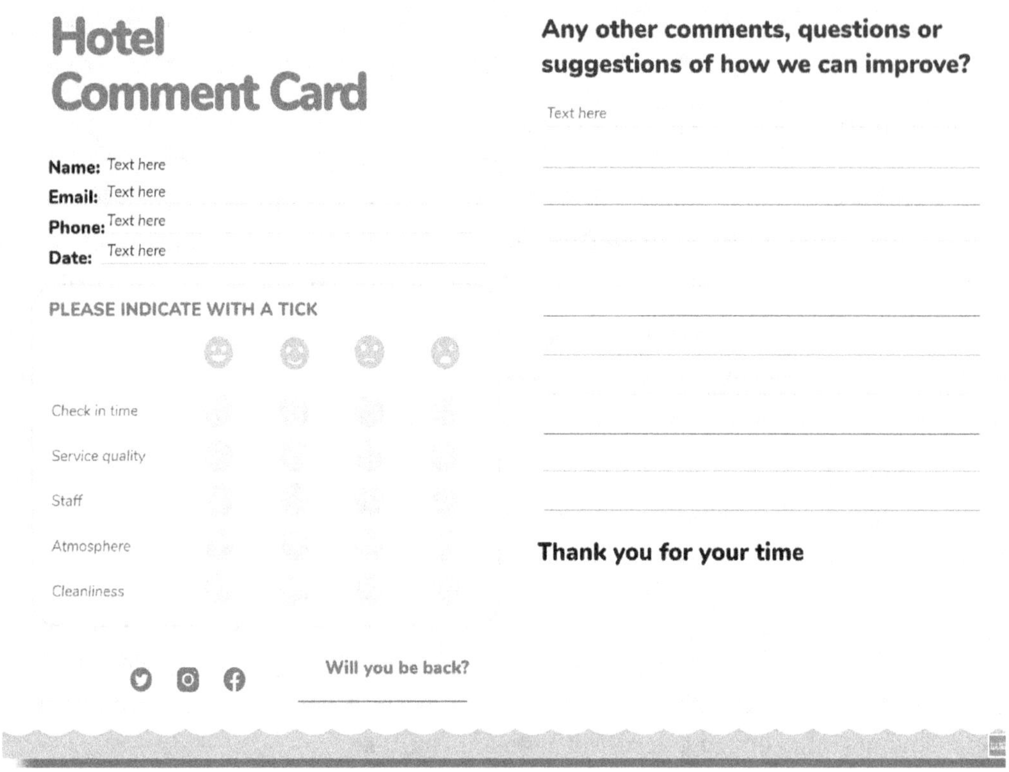

Hotel
Comment Card

Name: Text here
Email: Text here
Phone: Text here
Date: Text here

PLEASE INDICATE WITH A TICK

Check in time
Service quality
Staff
Atmosphere
Cleanliness

Will you be back?

Any other comments, questions or suggestions of how we can improve?

Text here

Thank you for your time

Figure 1

From my experience as both an employee and a customer, GCCs have never proven helpful. In some hotels I've worked in over the years, the same problems persist, along with the same furniture and even the same guests who have grown accustomed to both the positives and negatives. They are not returning guests from my perspective; they are merely the same customers. There are two different approaches here: the returning customer seeks improvements each time and returns for the enhanced experience, while the other type of customer is indifferent to improvements and merely needs a place to stay for another purpose, not necessarily enjoying the luxury of the surroundings.

I am not criticizing anyone, and every customer is respected, but hotels must understand that if a customer who offers no recommendations for improvement continues to exist, it suggests they do not care about such enhancements. Moreover, using outdated methods like GCCs signals to the customer that the hotel is not attentive either.

Therefore, hotels that survive in today's competitive landscape maintain good relationships with customers, a strategy known as relationship marketing. They engage with customers even after they depart by providing newsletters with new experiences or additions to the hotel, introducing new staff members who will take care of them next time, offering promotions, or adding new items to the F&B offerings. It's all about continuously caring for the customer, which ultimately enables hotels to increase their prices, Average Daily Rate (ADR), and Revenue per Available Room (RevPAR), calculated as the occupancy rate multiplied by the ADR. This approach also leads to longer guest stays, benefiting the hotel in multiple ways.

Customers now have different ways to provide feedback. They can complete surveys during their stay or meal and submit them before leaving the property. Feedback is not limited to just angry customers; managers also find value in receiving feedback to address any below-average experiences and enhance their venues.

Without a doubt, the digital era has given people more power by enabling them to share their opinions and experiences quickly and affordable with others. Customers have left insightful reviews on many well-known rating and review websites, such as Yelp, TripAdvisor, and OpenTable. Furthermore, people voice their ideas on well-known social media networks like Facebook and Twitter in addition to these specialized sites. It is imperative to recognize the enormous power that this client feedback possesses, since it may quickly and significantly affect organizations, considering that prospective customers frequently rely heavily on these websites and platforms when making judgments.

As unbelievable as it may seem, independent restaurants can achieve amazing results with simply a one-star change in their Yelp ratings. The thorough investigation carried out by Luca & Zervas produced an extremely fascinating finding: an increase in review site ratings unquestionably and considerably boosted the income streams of numerous eateries.

2. The Importance of ADR in the Hospitality Industry

As a result of the ever-increasing complexities and intricacies within the hospitality industry and the continually evolving digital era, the significance and value of ADR agreements have been elevated to the forefront. These agreements, unique in their nature, serve to compartmentalize and streamline "alternative" mechanisms that are specifically designed to effectively and efficiently resolve any disputes that may arise from the subject matter of contracts between commercial parties operating within this industry.

The core of these mechanisms revolves around two fundamental pillars: negotiation and mediation procedures. By incorporating these pillars, parties involved are not only able to avoid the often-adversarial approach of the conventional judicial process, but they also gain strategic advantages and cost-efficient benefits that can ultimately shape the trajectory of their businesses.

Here are some recent examples to highlight the importance of ADR agreements in the hospitality sector. Institutions like the International Society of Hospitality Consultants (ISHC) in the United States of America (USA) has stepped up to meet this vital need by offering tailored dispute resolution training programs to industry professionals. This initiative has assembled a team of seasoned arbitrators and mediators, combining their extensive expertise in addressing hospitality industry challenges. Consequently, the industry now boasts a pool of knowledgeable professionals, many of whom are current or former ISHC members with 10 to 40 years of hands-on experience. These individuals have undergone comprehensive training and certification as commercial arbitrators, mediators, and Issue Review Board members, ready to assist in resolving disputes ranging from straightforward to intricate. The ISHC, comprising over 200 members with diverse backgrounds spanning 60 countries, stands as a premier professional body. Membership is exclusive and by invitation, recognizing individuals as leaders in their respective fields. With expertise spanning more than 50 areas within the industry, ISHC offers a unique repository of global experience in hospitality.

On the other side of the Atlantic, ADR agreements are just as common. One of the best examples of ADR is the London Court of International Arbitration, which is located in the United Kingdom. This prestigious organization, which is well-known for its objectivity, reliability, and unparalleled experience, has played a crucial role in mediating several conflicts in the hospitality sector. Through the utilisation of arbitration, mediation, and negotiation, the London Court of International Arbitration fosters a constructive discourse that leads to just and fair resolutions.

In conclusion, ADR agreements have undeniably emerged as indispensable tools within the hospitality industry. By embracing mechanisms that promote collaborative problem-solving and minimize the burdensome complexities often associated with traditional judicial processes, commercial parties involved in this dynamic industry are able to navigate disputes seamlessly. With visionary institutions such as the Mississippi Gaming Commission and the London Court of International Arbitration leading the way, the future of ADR within the hospitality industry looks incredibly promising, ensuring the sustained growth and prosperity of this thriving sector.

Litigation is a time-consuming, costly, and unpredictable process, particularly where one or both parties are domiciled outside the jurisdiction where the courts are required to determine the dispute. The importance of providing commercial practicability by facilitating the fairest methods of structuring business relationships, such as ADR, is crucial to a thriving and growing hospitality industry. This importance has resulted in a paradigm shift from litigating disputes. Contrary to negotiation and mediation procedures, arbitration serves not only to streamline the dispute resolution process but also to provide a more structured environment to extract evidence and ultimately render a binding, enforceable award on a party in breach of its contractual obligations.

3. Examples of ADR in the Hospitality Industry

In the dynamic world of hospitality, where teams work tirelessly to ensure memorable guest experiences, conflicts between employees and management, as well as among colleagues, vendors and even the hotel operator with the hotel owners can occasionally emerge. These disputes, if left unaddressed, can undermine morale, disrupt operations, and tarnish the reputation of the establishment. Let's delve into a few scenarios where mediation plays a pivotal role in resolving such conflicts.

Reflecting on the case involving Sarah, Mike, and the hotel management, communication breakdowns and issues with task delegation emerge as the main causes of this strain. This frustrated employee begins contemplating airing their grievances on social media platforms, potentially damaging the hotel's reputation and standing. They feel neglected and under appreciated. Who would be the best person to settle this dispute? Or perhaps the department? Such situations often arise among coworkers, yet they remain concealed due to employment contracts. To impair matters, they all have personal responsibilities at home, including debts, loans, and other financial obligations, which occasionally hinder them from engaging in lengthy disputes. Nevertheless, their unresolved issues simmer beneath the surface, posing a risk of eruption at any moment, threatening their ability to reconcile. The toxic atmosphere threatens to permeate, affecting team morale and guest satisfaction, inevitably tarnishing the hotel's reputation and visitors' perceptions.

Some of these concerns may also follow the employee to another hotel or restaurant. The world of the hospitality industry is relatively small, where many individuals know each other either from training together, working together, or meeting at famous travel events such as the Arabian Travel Market (ATM) in Dubai or the World Travel Market (WTM). These events are major gatherings where hospitality leaders convene periodically to share insights and sometimes close deals. Imagine encountering an ex-colleague at such significant events during legal disputes; it could undoubtedly be embarrassing. Therefore, following the litigation process can sometimes hinder the progress of the industry and lead to conflicts between personnel, even after the litigation process concludes, leaving little room for individuals to transfer to reputable organizations due to minor conflicts that could have been mediated with amicable resolutions rather than litigation.

Additionally, mediation works well for settling disputes resulting from competition or apparent favouritism between coworkers. Disagreements concerning shift assignments or tip-sharing arrangements, for example, might worsen between kitchen personnel and servers in a restaurant, causing splits within the team. ADR methods can help to address these conflicts and find a mutually agreeable solution for all parties involved. Understanding how internal conflict affects customer service and operational effectiveness, restaurant management uses mediation to resolve the underlying issues that lead to conflict. Mediation sessions offer a safe environment where staff members may voice concerns, define goals, and come up with solutions that work for everyone while fostering cooperation and teamwork. This is due to the fact, as when one or both parties are domiciled outside of the jurisdiction where the courts are required to resolve the dispute, litigation can be a difficult, expensive, and uncertain procedure. A flourishing and expanding hotel industry depends on delivering commercial practicability through the facilitation of the fairest methods of organizing business interactions, such as ADR. Due to its significance, the practice of litigating disputes has changed. Unlike the processes of litigation, mediation and arbitration help to resolve disputes more quickly while also offering a more structured setting in which to gather evidence and, in the end, impose a legally binding verdict on a party that has violated the terms of the contract.

In the end, mediation is a fundamental component of dispute resolution in the hospitality sector, providing a positive substitute for confrontational methods. Through the promotion of transparent dialogue, understanding, and cooperation, mediation enables people to effectively handle interpersonal disputes, strengthen professional bonds, and maintain the common objective of providing outstanding guest experiences. In an industry where teamwork, hospitality, and guest satisfaction are paramount, the adoption of mediation as a proactive conflict resolution tool underscores a commitment to fostering a positive work culture and sustaining long-term success. Through mediation, hospitality establishments can cultivate resilient, cohesive teams that thrive in the face of challenges, enriching the guest experience and elevating their reputation in an ever-evolving landscape.

As a result, it can be said with confidence that ADR genuinely and successfully resolves a wide range of conflicts that may arise within the hospitality industry. ADR does this by skilfully and effectively offering a notably cost-effective and exceedingly efficient means of doing so. By using ADR, a wide range of disputes involving clients, staff, vendors, and other stakeholders can be handled quickly and effectively, resulting in a positive work environment and the ongoing provision of excellent services that are the industry standard.

CHAPTER FIVE
NAVIGATING DISPUTES IN MODERN HOSPITALITY

"Let there be justice for all. Let there be peace for all. Let there be work, bread, water, and salt for all."- Nelson Mandela

CHAPTER FIVE : NAVIGATING DISPUTES IN MODERN HOSPITALITY

Internal:

1. Employee Relations

Dispute scenario: Mike is an excellent employee who is engaged in different departments, and he actively handles the hotel telephone operator role during the afternoon shift, as discussed previously. Due to the perceived unfair treatment by management, and feeling undervalued in his critical role within the hotel, along with his salary remaining stagnant despite his efforts, Mike has begun gossiping and discussing the mistreatment of hotel staff, particularly himself, with his colleagues. Not only is he engaging in gossip, but he's also venting his frustrations and anger on his social media platforms. What implications might arise from this situation? How might this attitude affect his coworkers? Many questions regarding the selection of employees and management's treatment could arise in this scenario.

While many staff or employee issues may seem trivial, the truth is that many disputes can cost your hotel time, money, reputation, and even legal trouble. Disputes can involve wages, work schedules, or billing practices, as well as psychological bullying, cyber harassment, racial or gender discrimination, and sexual harassment. The novel corona virus pandemic has also led to issues with hazard pay and a hostile work environment, as employees experienced a lack of on-the-job safety provisions and retaliation against whistleblowers. Before hiring, it is important for hotel owners to conduct a background check for prospective staff members to prevent any potential legal problems down the road. In addition, implementing employment policies into the hotel operation strategy can help prevent the occurrence of new disputes by outlining how various employee relation situations will be handled or undertaken to ensure fair treatment among all staff members. The implementation of policies and procedures is crucial to preventing any disputes that can arise among employees within the hotel. These policies and procedures must be well-written and deployed, and they must also be flexible to change according to internal and external factors and environmental changes. Furthermore, these policies and procedures need to be relevant to the jurisdiction where the hotel is located. For example, a hotel under the same brand in the USA cannot adopt the same policy as one in another country in Asia or Africa, as legal systems and languages differ. Hotel operators can request assistance from a hospitality law firm or specialized legal firm in hospitality to draft policies and procedures tailored to each jurisdiction where the operator exists, drawing from their experience to avoid legal disputes and manage them within the organization. From my perspective, this may be the only time legal intervention can effectively address issues within the hospitality industry. This chapter will look at components that have an impact on these individuals in the organization as well.

1.1 Interpersonal Conflicts.

Interpersonal Relations (IR) is a third social network interaction that is formed through "individual perceptions, attitudes, and intentions" towards the other, "based on relationships among people and groups." Interpersonal relations, according to management theory, are seen as the most central in creating job satisfaction and motivation among employees. This, in turn, has an impact on many other aspects of performance in an organization, including commitment, customer service, and quality of service. One of the ways to improve on IR is to have employees "perceive support and fairness from the other team members and from the team supervisors." Theorists have long mentioned that forming friendships among employees would have a significant impact on positive organizational behavior. This is not just in maintaining employee relations but in creating a positive and friendly working environment as well.

At the heart of any business, in any sector, are the people. Management, staff, and customers are the invaluable assets that keep the business running and successful. The success of any business, including the hospitality industry, depends on focusing on these assets and ensuring that the business model does not isolate or segregate any of the stakeholders. The customer is seen as the essential part of the hospitality industry, bringing "life to any project," thus ensuring that customers' needs are put at the forefront of any plan. What about the relations between the two stakeholder groups in a hotel: the customers and the staff? Studies have shown that the same factors impacting the interpersonal relationships of employees also affect employees' relationships with customers. Some of the big names in the hospitality industry, such as Marriott, follow the simple motto "People first," which is the foundation of Marriott's corporate and cultural success. They believe if their people feel valued and trusted, their customers will too. I remember when I had a task force at JW Marriott in Dubai in 2009 (this hotel no longer exists due to some internal arrangements), the staff cafeteria food was equal to the guest food served in the restaurants, and even the staff accommodation was one of the best in the UAE at that time. This is how Marriott developed and evolved over the years and was able to acquire Starwood Hotels in 2016 after the stockholders of both Marriott International and Starwood Hotels and Resorts approved the merger. Imagine that even applying the policies and procedures on another well-known brand like Starwood, which was Marriott's main competitor in the market, is now applied to Starwood employees. I am not surprised that a hotel chain like Marriott can do so, as it emerged from its first hotel, the Twin Bridges Marriott Motor Hotel, in Arlington, Virginia, in 1957 to a total of 1,597,000 rooms and 7,000 hotels in 2023 in 139 countries and territories with 196 million members of the Marriott Bonvoy loyalty program. How did they do it? It's all about people because People first![15]

1.2 Work-related Grievances.

In disputes between management and employees, workers would do well to remember how difficult it is for companies to document performance problems in a consistent and defensible way. When a worker is terminated, a human resources (HR) department can easily go back through hiring records to verify that the fired worker has had issues all along, but the opposite is often true when a worker is terminated. In fact, supervisors of employees who are eventually fired often lack documentation of low performance and may struggle to provide evidence supporting their decision. No matter who is right or wrong, when there are disputes between you and a supervisor, there can be severe consequences for you (if the supervisor is right), the company, and even your union. A lack of properly handled disciplines and terminations can lead to the monopoly of complaints because everyone is unhappy with the status quo and justifiably so, or no complaints whatsoever from an unengaged and disheartened workforce because of the pattern of inaction.

Tensions can rise, productivity can fall, and a toxic work environment can become the norm. Work-related grievances can take many forms, including unfair treatment, harassment, and discrimination, all of which can significantly impact employees' well-being and job satisfaction. These negative effects can manifest in various ways, such as increased stress levels, decreased motivation, and a decline in overall mental health. Moreover, the consequences extend beyond the individual employee, as a toxic work environment can also lead to higher turnover rates, decreased team cohesion, and ultimately, hinder the organization's success. Therefore, it is crucial for employers to prioritize creating a positive and inclusive work culture that fosters open communication, respects diversity, and actively addresses any potential grievances. By doing so, employers can create a safe and supportive environment that promotes employee well-being, engagement, and ultimately, organizational growth.

---

[15] Marriott International. IV. Corporate History. Marriott International. 2022. https://www.marr ott.com/marriottassets/marriott/MI/CorporateHistory.pdf. [Accessed: February. 29, 2024]

1.3 Misunderstandings.

No public place is more famous for misunderstandings than hotel in-room dining. For example, a guest orders a cheeseburger, but the staff member brings the burger without the cheese after a 30-minute wait. The staff apologizes and promises to get a proper cheeseburger, but when he returns 10 minutes later, the burger is cold. Frustrated, the guest asks to cancel the order and refuses to pay. The order taker informs the duty manager, who calls the guest to discuss the problem. Instead of resolving the issue, this adds another layer of frustration as the guest has to repeat his order. The duty manager struggles to hear him, asking the guest to lower his voice and stop shouting. The guest hangs up, and now an hour passed without a resolution. The duty manager, who is responsible for handling such cases daily, is also frustrated and overlooks the guest's request. The next morning, the duty manager finds that the guest has made a comment on TripAdvisor about the entire incident. This situation raises questions about the implementation of policies and procedures, training, and the skills of the duty manager in handling difficult situations.

Misunderstandings, miscommunications, misinterpretations, and errors can also lead to disputes. It's all about the operator or hotel management effectively implementing its policies and procedures and monitoring their execution among all staff members. The hotel's reputation and profits depend on the right implementation of these policies and procedures across all employees and staff members. Problems in hotels often arise when the General Manager (GM) is perceived as being above all limits, solely responsible for monitoring implementation, and not subject to the same rules, as he has the authority to hire and fire based on his perspective. Some hotels, especially individual brand hotels, operate this way, often managed by the owner himself or sometimes with an inexperienced GM who lacks the knowledge and skills to read financial statements and advise accordingly on Key Performance Indicators (KPIs). Consequently, the productivity of each department and the associated costs, along with the implementation of policies and procedures, suffer. Forming a committee of department heads to revise and implement a unified standard for policies and procedures can be crucial for individual hotels. This approach helps them stand out in a competitive market, avoid disputes, and reduce employee turnover over time.

2. Management-Stakeholder Relations.

2.1 Stakeholders Success strategies.

Stakeholder collaboration is vital for the success of any hospitality business. Imagine a well-orchestrated symphony where each musician plays a unique instrument, yet all harmonize to create a beautiful performance. Management sets the rhythm with strategic planning, employees add the melody with their attentive service, suppliers contribute the harmony by providing quality products, and the local community enriches the performance with its unique cultural notes. When all these stakeholders work together seamlessly, they create an exceptional experience for guests, ensuring satisfaction and a competitive edge in the hospitality industry. This collaboration not only enhances guest experiences but also strengthens the entire business, making it resilient and innovative.

To foster effective stakeholder collaboration and avoid disputes, several strategies are essential. First, implementing comprehensive training and development programs for all staff members is crucial. These programs should cover customer service, conflict resolution, and cultural sensitivity to ensure that employees can handle various situations professionally and respectfully. Additionally, defining clear goals and objectives for each staff member helps in preventing misunderstandings. Regular feedback and inclusive decision-making processes further enhance this clarity, ensuring everyone understands their roles and responsibilities.

Creating a collaborative work environment where employees feel like real stakeholders is crucial for any hospitality business. For instance, imagine a hotel that implements open communication channels and inclusive decision-making processes. Here, employees from all levels can voice their ideas and concerns during regular team meetings, contributing to important decisions about hotel operations and guest services. This honest dialogue fosters a sense of ownership and collective effort, where every team member feels valued and invested in the hotel's success. Such an environment not only boosts morale and productivity but also enhances the overall guest experience, as employees are more motivated to go above and beyond in their roles.

Taking Emaar Properties as an example[16], an Emirati multinational real estate development company, exemplifies how a successful public listed company in the hospitality industry can thrive through innovative employee engagement strategies. Based in the United Arab Emirates, Emaar's largest shareholders include Dubai ruler Mohammed bin Rashid Al Maktoum and the UAE's sovereign wealth fund, the Investment Corporation of Dubai. As a public joint-stock company listed on the Dubai Financial Market, Emaar has a valuation of US$16.8 billion as of August 2023, with a Net Asset Valuation of US$37.6 billion (AED 138.1B) as of December 2022, according to third-party valuations. Emaar is renowned for its landmark projects, including the world-famous Burj Khalifa.

Emaar Hospitality Group, the hotel division of Emaar Properties, manages a portfolio of luxury hotels and resorts that attract millions of guests worldwide. A cornerstone of Emaar's strategy is creating a collaborative work environment where employees feel like real stakeholders. One effective method Emaar employs is the Employees' Performance Share Programme. This programme fosters a sense of ownership and directly aligns employees' interests with the company's success. By having a stake in the company, employees are motivated to go above and beyond in their roles, contributing to the overall success of the hotel operations. For example, consider a situation where a guest suggests adding more vegan options to the menu. In Emaar's hotels, such feedback could be discussed in team meetings that include staff from various departments—kitchen, front desk, and management. By encouraging open communication and inclusive decision-making, the team can evaluate the feasibility and benefits of the suggestion from multiple perspectives. If the idea is implemented, it not only improves the guest experience but also gives employees a sense of contribution and achievement.

Additionally, Emaar ensures that its policies and procedures are effectively implemented and monitored across all staff members, maintaining high standards of service and operation. The performance share programme further enhances this by incentivizing employees to adhere to these standards, knowing that their efforts directly impact the company's stock performance and, consequently, their compensation. The Nomination and Remuneration Committee at Emaar plays a vital role in supporting this collaborative environment. The main objectives and responsibilities of the committee include regulating and supervising procedures for the nomination of Board members, identifying and reviewing candidates for senior management positions, and making recommendations for appointments. The committee also reviews the Board structure, size, and composition to ensure compliance with applicable laws and makes necessary adjustments. It determines the executive management and employee needs and criteria for their selection, ensuring that the methods applied are in accordance with the law.

Furthermore, the committee issues and supervises the implementation of HRs and training policies, reviewing these policies annually. It also formulates a remuneration policy covering bonuses, benefits, incentives, and salaries for Board members and employees, ensuring these packages reflect the performance and circumstances of various business units in different markets and countries. The committee administers Emaar's share option schemes for Group executives and directors, aligning their interests with those of

---

16 Emaar Sukuk Limited, "Base Prospectus," Emaar Sukuk Limited, Aug. 31, 2016 [Online]

the company and its shareholders. The Nomination and Remuneration Committee meets annually and as needed, complying with Securities and Commodities Authority (SCA) regulations, and fulfilling its outlined objectives and responsibilities.

This collaborative approach not only enhances employee morale and productivity but also creates a positive and engaging atmosphere for guests. Emaar's strategy of treating employees as stakeholders through the Employees' Performance Share Programme is a key factor behind its continued success and reputation for excellence in the competitive hospitality industry. Moreover, linking part of employee compensation to company performance through stock options can motivate employees to perform at their best and foster a sense of ownership and loyalty. By integrating these practices, hotels can create a harmonious and efficient workplace, preventing disputes and ensuring all stakeholders are engaged and invested in the business's success.

2.2 Financial Matters.

In the dynamic realm of the hospitality industry, Whether it's a hotel, restaurant, bar, or events company, all of the hospitality sector faces similar challenges when it comes to keeping cash flowing. Monthly financial landscapes vary significantly, with revenue streams ebbing and flowing, and seasonal shifts being the norm. Economic pressures have worsened the already demanding trading conditions faced by these businesses. Foremost among the concerns of every business owner are energy bills, which pose a significant financial burden, particularly for hospitality enterprises. The complexity of lighting and heating expansive premises has heightened, leaving many businesses anxious about coping with escalating utility expenses.

Securing suitable locations for hotels, restaurants, or event spaces is crucial, yet obtaining funding through traditional bank loans often proves challenging, necessitating the search for appropriate mortgages tailored to the business's needs. Essential kitchen equipment and furnishings for dining areas and accommodations entail substantial financial investments for hotels and restaurants. Additionally, the inclusion of amenities such as gyms or spas, while enhancing guest experiences, adds to the financial strain with initial setup and ongoing maintenance costs. Seasonal demand fluctuations in the hospitality sector lead to periods of peak activity followed by quieter spells, causing financial constraints during off-peak times. These constraints, coupled with persistent bills, wages, and expenses, necessitate robust funding solutions to navigate leaner periods.

For example, consider a trendy downtown restaurant, renowned for its mouthwatering cuisine and stylish ambiance, but struggling to secure the perfect location for expansion. As it seeks to broaden its culinary footprint, traditional bank loans fall short, prompting the restaurateur to explore alternative financing options tailored to its unique needs.

Now, picture a luxurious mountain resort, where guests indulge in pampering spa treatments and gourmet dining experiences. Behind the scenes, the resort grapples with the hefty investment required to maintain top-of-the-line kitchen equipment and furnish its elegant dining spaces. Additionally, the allure of a world-class spa comes with the ongoing financial commitment of upkeep and maintenance.

As the seasons change, so does the rhythm of hospitality. During the bustling summer months, hotels and restaurants hum with activity, while the quieter winter season brings financial challenges. For a boutique hotel nestled in a charming village, navigating the leaner months requires careful financial planning to cover bills, wages, and expenses without compromising on guest experience.

Among these financial ebbs and flows, the hospitality industry faces another pressing challenge: a shortage of skilled workers. Imagine a bustling hotel lobby buzzing with activity, where the front desk struggles to find qualified staff to greet guests with warmth and professionalism. The scarcity of skilled workers drives up wages, adding to the financial strain on hospitality businesses already grappling with other financial burdens.

The culmination of these challenges can potentially escalate into disputes and lengthy legal proceedings, posing significant challenges to hotels. Disagreements over financial obligations, contract terms, and resource management may arise, leading to protracted legal battles that drain both financial and HRs. These disputes can disrupt operations, tarnish reputations, and strain relationships with stakeholders, making it imperative for hotels to proactively address financial challenges and seek effective resolution mechanisms to avoid prolonged legal entanglements.

2.3 Business Direction.

The hospitality industry can sometimes resemble the Titanic, boasting impressive features but lacking clear direction. This includes businesses within the sector such as hotels, restaurants, bars, casinos, and clubs. Why does this happen? It can be attributed to poor management decisions or external factors like political, environmental, social, technological, and logistical elements (PESTLE). The hospitality industry is uniquely competitive, with prices fluctuating daily based on occupancy rates despite the market conditions.

For instance, consider an Indian wedding ceremony that lasts a week. In early 2023, Rixos Premium Seagate and Rixos Sharm El Sheikh hosted their first-ever Indian wedding in Egypt. Organized by Inventum Global and Jaydeep, president of EMF ACE, this event saw 450 guests enjoying Rixos' legendary hospitality over three days and nights. The event featured impeccable service, stunning decor, and breathtaking views. To enhance the experience, 200 Indian staff, including 50 chefs, brought 2,300 kg of equipment and food, infusing the celebration with authentic Indian flavors. Performances by the Indian Pop Rock Band Sanam, artist Armaan Malik, and renowned singer Neha Kakkar made it an unforgettable celebration.

Imagine the revenue generated by such an event, with guests occupying not only rooms but also restaurants, bars, and every facility of the hotel. Meanwhile, other hotels in the same city might have expected less revenue during that time. This disparity highlights the importance of brand reputation, with Rixos being one of the top brands in the hotel sector, offering rates not affordable for everyone and hiring the best staff to meet guest needs. However, these top-tier staff require higher budgets, especially foreign staff paid in USD while the local currency is Egyptian pounds.

Consider how many similar weddings could occur in a year following this event and the potential revenue. It may not always be the same, prompting hotel management to reconsider their staffing budgets. Many hotel strategies involve hiring the best staff to drive revenue, but this approach should be balanced with monthly business volume, market segments, and guest demographics. Failure to consider these factors can lead to disputes and legal issues.

EXTERNAL.

1. **Owner-Operator Hotel Management Agreements.**

1.1   *Overview of Owner-Operator Hotel Management Agreements.*

The hotel operating company manages the commercial aspect of the hotel in which the operating company generates a return in excess of management fees, however sometimes disputes arise between the Owner who is typically a group of investors that together form a legal entity referred to as a Special Purpose Entity (SPE) created solely for the purpose of a hotel operating partnership for that single property (the "Owner") and the hotel operating company (the "Operator") regarding contractual obligations, profit sharing, or performance metrics. The Hotel Management Agreement (HMA) is sophisticated; it covers revenue management, marketing and reports, the safety and security of guests and employees alike, and employer/employee relations in real time and dispute resolution clause, among other things. Knowing that, disputes can be at inception when the HMA is drafted, they can arise at execution, or over time while the property is being managed. In the upcoming points we will address the HMA within the context of the external influences that affects the terms and conditions of the HMA from the owner and operator perspectives.

Disputes in the hospitality industry are not uncommon, particularly in the context of Owner-Operator HMA. These agreements, which govern the relationship between the Owner and the Operator, can give rise to various conflicts and challenges throughout their life cycle. Understanding the nature and causes of these disputes is crucial in order to effectively address and mitigate them. In this chapter, we will explore the key issues surrounding disputes in Owner-Operator HMA's and their implications for both parties involved.

The owner-operator hotel management agreement is the underlying contract by which the purposes of the owner, typically to maximize the profits and get a good return on investment, furthermore the Operator will typically provide the necessary expertise and resources to operate the hotel. This contract, when not properly negotiated, can lead to conflicts of interest between the two parties involved. It is of utmost importance that Owners thoroughly review and evaluate the agreement, taking into consideration all the terms and conditions. Likewise, Operators should also dedicate the necessary time and effort to examine the contract, ensuring fairness, transparency, and clarity in all aspects. By doing so, both parties can foster an environment of collaboration and synergy to extract the maximum value and potential from the hotel, thus driving its success and profitability to new heights.

In the first place, we must consider that the acquisition of the property and the establishment of the hotel itself are complex operations. The owner will have to take senior management measures with the goal of maximizing the profits from the hotel and obtaining an adequate return on investment. With this concept in mind, the owner will have to decide on the best management formula for them and the property. The owner must select an operator who can optimize the property's performance for many years. This operator must have the experience that the owner needs to ensure the successful operation and financial performance of the hotel.

Most hotels are owned by companies or individual owners who have prior experience in the industry, either through owning other properties, or having some involvement in the sector. These property owners have the flexibility to choose from a range of management options for their hotel. However, this decision is not as straightforward as it may seem. Owners must carefully assess various factors, including financial considerations, legal obligations, and the level of control they desire over the operation. Similarly, operators must consider factors such as the terms and conditions outlined in the agreement, the reputation of the brand, the available resources, and the ongoing relationship with the owner. This is particularly important if the owner possesses different properties in different jurisdictions that the operator may have an interest in.

1.2 *Common Disputes in Owner-Operator Hotel Management Agreements.*

Owner-operators will always have disputes, some of which are totally independent of the operator who will bear the added cost. The number of disputes that result in litigation is greatly reduced because of the Operator's vast experience. Even when the Operator prevails, the Operator is still a loser because of the huge legal costs and negative publicity. One such resolution alternative is filing for arbitration. Currently, Owner-Operator agreements generally provide for binding arbitration for unresolved disputes. Some of the larger dispute firms that routinely work with the large hotel management companies include the American Arbitration Association, the International Center of Dispute Resolution (ICDR), Judicate West, JAMS, Resolute Mediation & Arbitration Inc., as well as the University of Houston. While filing for arbitration may indeed shorten the process, it will not eliminate the cost for the following reasons:.

Disputes in the hospitality industry are an everyday occurrence that can test the resilience and efficiency of any establishment. Due to the intricacies and extensive nature of larger properties, the likelihood of disputes arising significantly increases. These conflicts can span a wide spectrum, encompassing employee-related matters, contractual disagreements, labor disputes, delivery discrepancies, damages to life and property, and even guest complaints that touch on hygiene standards, perceived fairness, or the unfortunate release of compromising videos.

It is vital for such conflicts to be resolved promptly and effectively, as the consequences of allowing them to fester or escalate to court can be financially and reputationally devastating. Thankfully, there exist various avenues through which disputes can be methodically tackled and peace can be restored. Some of the most commonly employed methods include mediation, arbitration, ombudsman processes, engaging a party-neutral expert, initiating the legal process by filing a lawsuit, or resorting to executive negotiation.

Overall, prioritizing the resolution of disputes is of utmost importance in the hospitality industry. By swiftly addressing conflicts and employing appropriate methods of reconciliation, establishments can maintain harmony, foster positive relationships, and secure their standing as providers of exceptional service.

1.2.1 *Disagreements over financial responsibilities.*

HMA's dictate the rights and obligations between Owners and Operators. An HMA allocates the responsibilities and tasks concerning day-to-day hotel operations. Furthermore, an HMA determines who has control over a host of business-related matters. In the event that contract execution causes ambiguity or conflict, an HMA can be arbitrated. An HMA can be as long as fifty or more pages. Portions of this document will pertain to compensation and operational performance, such as the base management fee; the incentive management fee, offsite fees (booking and reservation fees); income from ancillary operations and special charges; reimbursement of food and beverage service, other catering costs, or non-special charges; and the allocation of costs, commissions, and rebates. Court case arbitration of hotel management agreement disputes has existed long enough to extract trends in those disagreements.

Hotel operators and owners may encounter various challenges and unforeseen circumstances, but not all of them necessarily result in disputes. While arbitration is a frequently used method for resolving legal conflicts, it may not play a significant role in every case between the two parties. It is important to find a way to ensure the hotel management agreement (HMA) continues for the duration of the contract. Additionally, the hotel operator may have also signed agreements with the same or different owners in other jurisdictions. In this situation, terminating the agreement due to minor issues that can be resolved through effective communication and negotiation might not be the first choice for the operator.

1.2.2 *Disputes regarding property maintenance and renovations.*

The responsibility for installing and managing hotel facilities is an important question. The HMA outlines the specific duties and authority of the hotel manager. Additionally, there are laws related to the hotel industry and real estate lease laws that have specific regulations for hotel management. The HMA typically includes responsibilities for hotel construction, extensions, repairs, and replacements for various types of properties. Therefore, it is necessary to establish a procedure in a standard HMA to determine the need for repairs, the specific repair requirements, and the terms when a hotel has been in operation for a certain period of time. However, even if a management agreement does not explicitly specify repair procedures and requirements, the hotel manager still has an obligation to address them.

Failure to adequately maintain and renovate the property can result in disagreements between the Owner and the Operator, potentially leading to legal action or the termination of the management agreement. In these situations, the Owner may argue that the Operator's lack of attention to property upkeep and renovations has negatively affected the property's value and reputation. For instance, if a fire occurs in the kitchen due to the chef's failure to turn off the gas stations, this is not considered an force majeure situation, but rather a result of negligence. The Operator may request the Owner to cover the costs of the damage, however, the Owner argues that the Operator should be responsible for the damages as the fire was caused by the kitchen team's negligence and the Operator should bear the expenses from their operational budget. If such issues are not addressed in legally binding clauses, disputes can arise. Owners and Operators should ensure that their contractual agreements contain clear and specific clauses to prevent such disputes, allowing for discussions on other matters that are more beneficial to both parties instead focusing on resolving losses.

1.2.3 *Conflicts related to staffing and employment.*

During the term of a Hotel Management Agreement (HMA), there is often a practical discrepancy of interest between the owner and the operator regarding the staffing of hotel employees. The operator typically seeks the flexibility to adjust staffing levels as deemed necessary to maintain the hotel and brand standards stipulated in the HMA. This is crucial for the operator, as maintaining brand standards is directly linked to the hotel's reputation and operational efficiency. The operator benefits from having adequate staff to ensure smooth hotel operations and uphold the brand image.

Conversely, the owner is primarily interested in minimizing operating expenses, especially when the hotel's performance falls below budget expectations. The owner's focus is on maximizing revenue and profit, which sometimes conflicts with the operator's priority of sustaining the brand image and quality of service. For instance, while the owner might prefer to reduce staffing to cut costs, the operator might insist on maintaining or even increasing staff levels to ensure that the hotel meets its operational standards and guest expectations.

Consider the operator's standard that requires one housekeeping staff member for every ten rooms. In scenarios of high occupancy or overbooking, this standard becomes particularly challenging. The operator must decide whether to adhere to this staffing ratio, which might necessitate hiring additional temporary staff, or to manage with fewer employees, which could compromise service quality. This decision is further complicated when the hotel is booked through various channels, such as travel agencies offering discounted rates and online travel agencies (OTAs) with higher rates. The operator must balance the staffing needs to serve guests from both sources effectively.

For example, if a significant number of rooms are booked at lower rates through travel agencies, the operator might be tempted to reduce staff to save costs. However, doing so could result in poor service, leading to guest dissatisfaction and negative reviews on platforms like TripAdvisor. Negative reviews can severely impact the hotel's reputation and future bookings, highlighting the importance of adequate staffing despite lower immediate revenue from discounted rates.

The operator's expertise in handling such situations is crucial, and the owner must understand and support the operator's decisions to maintain service standards. Monthly or quarterly budget meetings should involve open communication and a shared understanding of these operational challenges. Owners should avoid rigidly challenging the budget during these meetings, as inflexible cost-cutting measures can lead to more significant issues, such as guest complaints and a tarnished brand image.

Ultimately, the goal is to find a balance that satisfies both parties. The operator should demonstrate how maintaining proper staffing levels contributes to long-term profitability through enhanced guest satisfaction and loyalty. The owner, on the other hand, should appreciate the operational complexities and trust the operator's judgment in staffing decisions to ensure the hotel's success.

1.2.4 *Disagreements on marketing and branding strategies*

Branding has long been recognized as crucial in the hotel industry, but the effects of branding on dispute frequency in the HMA structure have yet to be studied. In my experience, the operator's brand is the key factor that allows the owner to engage with the operator in an HMA. For example, Marriott, Accor, Hilton, and IHG are considered big names that any owner would be proud to be associated with. According to the brand, the operator decides on the pricing scheme throughout the year. It could happen that the hotel is situated in a location where the prices are not so high and are affordable to guests, but the brand sends a message to the guest that what you pay is what you get, and the brand reputation is reflected in the overall guest experience.

Therefore, I have not experienced disputes between owners and operators solely based on the brand. Only if the owner finds that the rates implemented on some days are equal to or matching the competition's rates, the owner may interfere and ask why a big brand is diluting its rates in the market while other individual brands are able to maintain higher rates. However, these kinds of disputes are more often resolved amicably in their frequent meetings with a clear explanation of the revenue management. As long as the hotel is able to maintain and reach the budget, the owner has no right to interfere in the hotel operation, except if other hotels are reaching higher revenues, this usually the operator point of view.

This can be determined by some Key Performance Indicators (KPIs) such as the Revenue Generated Index (RGI) or the Market Penetration Index (MPI). These KPIs determine the position of the hotel amongst their competition, even if the hotel has reached its monthly budget. Here, sometimes disputes may arise, but they are still manageable.

However, disputes almost always arise in the branding area when a hotel is classified as a five-star hotel and the hotel operator agreed that it would be a five-star. But when the operator is about to execute the branding, the hotel is found to be sold as a four-star hotel. Now the owner wonders what this is for, and the operator replies that although the hotel has a five-star classification, it is a non-alcoholic hotel and cannot be classified as a five-star hotel. It will not have such premium rates if it is sold as a five-star hotel among the competition, and it can even lose its market share and affect the brand image. But what about the HMA and all related activities? Here it becomes a dispute where the operator does not accept having this brand with higher rates according to the market as it lacks the facilities, despite the authorities' classification, and the owner does not accept having his asset diluted.

If these kinds of disputes go to court, it may take years to have a decision, knowing that the courts sometimes lack understanding of the commercial aspects of the entire agreement. Therefore, they need to hire an expert in the field to determine the exact problem. So, if the court would hire an expert to determine the problem and report it to the courts, why did the parties not work on ADR instead of the courts? It may have been faster and quicker in terms of the decision since an expert was going to be hired anyway.

Sometimes the market conditions and the competition can externally define the hotel pricing despite its classification. Even sometimes, when the hotel operator's term is finished, maybe after 15 years, they begin thinking about renovation to match the existing brand image. Sometimes the owner will not accept it as he may not have gotten the profits needed along the contract term. Here, the operator may seek to go for a less prestigious brand. This operation will usually affect the customer, as the customer is clever and will know that this hotel is not the same brand anymore. There is no need to visit as they will know that it is not as competitive as it used to be.

2. Best Practices for Avoiding and Resolving Disputes

A good business relationship begins with setting it up properly. The time to address issues before they become disputes is when the parties are engaged in negotiating the hotel management agreement. Implementing the following five steps during the contract negotiation can help avoid future disputes. Owners should start by entering into a hotel management agreement with a hotel operator they know and trust. Owners should be clearly and candidly evaluate the operator's interest in a management agreement. The operator will be more inclined to make the management agreement work if the operator has a strong incentive to do so. Of course, like any deal term, the incentive package should be reasonable and market-based.

2.1 Clear and comprehensive contract drafting

First, a comprehensive contract includes all the provisions precisely tailored to the reality and specific characteristics of the hotel property. Before mutualizing an existing contract by copying and pasting it, as soon as possible, the Owners and the Operators must, of course, see each other to be able to observe what will bring them closer together. But more frequently, they must discuss separately within a small committee meeting. That is, on the one hand, a working group composed exclusively of owners and their consultants, and on the other hand, a substance of the property and the operator and their respective lawyers who are not only understand the legal terms but also talk commercial and understand the intricacies of the industry (which is drastically important for both parties). This working group brings together everyone who knows the property well and can express a specific point of view, particularly in terms of zoning, building, decoration, and revenue management.

Results: Disputes in the hospitality industry. In short, there are necessarily different attitudes regarding these agreements. The Owners and Operators are more interested in making the most while limiting their commitments, while the Operators will seek a perfect balance between the protection of their interests and more flexibility. To resolve these differences, it is essential to proceed with clear and comprehensive drafting of the contract, paying close attention to its key provisions, which are at the heart of managing the relationship between the two parties. While the words "clear" and "comprehensive" may be perceived as synonymous, they have different meanings when drafting a contract. Clear refers to the contract being easily understood and free from ambiguity, while comprehensive means that the contract covers all necessary aspects and leaves no room for interpretation.

2.2 Regular communication and performance monitoring

Owners generally prefer to have frequent and detailed communication from Operators. This helps to prevent challenges and disputes, or resolve them at an earlier stage when they are easier to manage. To achieve this, Owners can have their own experts in areas like revenue management contracts or even a commercial driven lawyer. It is also important for Owners to receive regular financial reports to stay updated on the performance of their operation. Additionally, making regular visits to the hotel allows Owners to assess the property's condition. According to a report, eight out of ten major brand franchisers emphasized the need for detailed benchmarking data and financial goals/results in the contract. This ensures that both parties have a clear understanding of the performance expectations and can address any discrepancies in a timely manner.

Regular communication and performance monitoring are crucial for maintaining a strong relationship between Owners and Operators in the hospitality industry. Owners and Operators should have regular meetings to discuss performance metrics, identify areas of improvement, and address any concerns or issues.

2.3 Establishing dispute resolution procedures upfront

Hotel managers understand that during the lifespan of the HMA, there will likely be conflict or certain provisions that will need to be amended or renegotiated. An essential component of a successful HMA is to include provisions for meetings of the parties to aim to resolve issues. It is important to discuss management dispute resolution procedures in the abstract – not in relation to any particular disputes that are current. Often, management can persuade a hotel Owner to agree to a new approach if they are not distracted by defending their corner in a particular dispute and being given an opportunity to suggest their own ideas. In order to ensure that disputes are not prolonged and resolved in a timely and cost-effective manner, it is advisable for the parties to include an ADR clause in the hotel management agreement.

Disputes are often highly complex, and there is always the potential for relationships to become toxic during the negotiation process. Accordingly, it is advisable for the parties to agree upfront on the procedures that should apply should a disagreement arise, ideally during the scoping and selection stages of the prospective agreement. In the absence of procedures to deal with disputes, parties may default to the litigation process rather than considering ADR processes. Indeed, most modern hotel management agreements are written with a sophisticated arbitration process in order to contain legal costs and ensure a relative degree of confidentiality, with management disclosing the least private aspects of their hotel operations. It should be noted that even when the HMA stipulates that disputes should follow an arbitration process, it is still open to either party not to invoke these procedures, thereby reverting to another ADR process such as mediation or negotiation, based on mutual agreement.

2.4 Seeking legal advice and counsel

Even in the best economic conditions, involvement in a dispute or litigation is not an activity that a party anticipates with glee, and it is not fun for legal counsel either. But by taking a proactive approach to the initial transaction and seeking specialized legal advice in the event of a dispute, the likelihood of reaching a resolution that is fair to all parties is far greater. "An ounce of prevention is worth a pound of cure." On the other hand, when hotels and other hospitality properties are well run, they provide an unforgettable experience. Hotels that operate well under a recognizable flag are typically not operating by mistake; instead, carefully executed business decisions and the implementation of those business decisions are often responsible. A well-run and profitable business operating under a brand managed by parties who treat each other fairly and in a way that encourages the exchange of ideas, is a recipe for success.

If a party finds itself in a dispute, or a party becomes involved in litigation, it is imperative to seek specialized legal advice and counsel from someone with expertise in the area of the dispute and who is well versed in the hospitality industry. An attorney should be consulted who has the requisite expertise in the subject matter of the dispute (e.g. hospitality, culinary, franchise, insurance), who is reputable and specialized, who has practical/industry and general commercial litigation experience, and who will research and be up-to-date on the law. An attorney who invests in educating himself or herself about the parties' businesses and the industry is invaluable. It is important to share all of the pertinent documents and information with counsel so that counsel can evaluate the situation fully and make recommendations accordingly. The cost of prosecuting or defending a matter should be discussed and understood in advance of engagement.

2.5 Maintaining a cooperative and collaborative relationship

Second, and closely related to the first point, the decision to enter into a hotel venture should be viewed as an economically rational decision that offers benefits to both the owner and the operator of the hotel. Simply put, no project will work if it is structured so that the owner fails; equally, if the owner performs well, so should the operator. Fostering such an economically rational approach requires that the Owner and Operator act in what the tensions or incentives, even if they separately work to their own benefit, should be conducive to behaviour that fosters long-term relationships between the parties. This is not to say that both parties ought not to act in their own business interests, but doing so in a way that is not "just for me" can, and should, be designed to also be "just for us". Data shows that the most successful arrangements between professional hotel managements – whether they are operating a 325-room five-star in London or a 25-room limited service in Syracuse, New York – have the same focus: do what is right for the customer (whose interest is represented by the brand owner), and the details of the agreement can be worked out to ensure mutual success.

Informative tone:

It is important for the parties involved to consider a few sensible approaches in order to maintain a long-term, successful partnership. Cooperation and collaboration are key attributes of a good partnership, and they are likely to contribute to the longevity of the relationship. Both the Owner and the Operator should devote time and effort to understanding each other's needs, goals, and constraints. Assuming that the other party is unconcerned or unaware of these factors can lead to conflicts and disagreements. On the other hand, acknowledging and accepting each other's needs and limitations, and recognizing that neither party is exclusively equipped to make the most effective decisions regarding the structure and management of the business, can foster constructive and collaborative discussions about problems and potential solutions.

3. **Resolution Mechanisms for Disputes.**

Effective mechanisms for resolving disputes within the HMAs are crucial for ensuring smooth operations and maintaining positive relationships between owners and operators in the hospitality industry. The HMAs should clearly outline the process for resolving disputes, including specifying the types of disputes subject to international arbitration and the location of arbitration tribunals. Additionally, defining the criteria for issuing a notice of dispute and determining its recipients ensures transparency and efficiency in conflict resolution. Collaborative discussions during the negotiation phase of the agreement can provide valuable insights into regulating the HMA, contributing to its effectiveness in managing disputes.

Disputes are an essential aspect of any business relationship, emphasizing the need for efficient resolution strategies within HMAs. In scenarios where commitments and obligations lack specificity, collaborative efforts between executive employees and boards of directors are crucial to clarify and streamline operational duties. Provisions within the HMA, such as those addressing transfer and termination clauses, serve to safeguard shareholders' interests, particularly in the event of operational failure. Clear notice of dispute protocols is essential to prevent procedural delays and costly legal battles, especially concerning disputes arising from operational strategy changes or breaches of service standards.

The effectiveness of dispute resolution mechanisms outlined in HMAs directly impacts the stability and success of hospitality ventures. Failure to adhere to these agreements can result in prolonged legal proceedings, financial strain, and strained relationships between parties. Disputes over the obligations of both the owner and the operator obligations towards each other, under performance, or breaches of service standards may trigger termination clauses, jeopardizing the reputation and profitability of the hotel. Therefore, a thorough understanding, and implementation of the dispute resolution procedures outlined in HMAs are essential for promoting harmony and mitigating conflicts within the hospitality industry. These mechanisms ensure that disputes are addressed promptly and fairly, minimizing disruptions to business operations and preserving the integrity of the contractual agreements. But what kind of resolution mechanisms that should the operator and the owner should implement during conflicts? Should they rely on litigation directly or should they use other effective resolution mechanisms to avoid such prolonged litigation process?.

1.1 Negotiation

In determining the effective resolution mechanism, I personally believe that negotiation is part of any successful relationship between the owner and the operator. Both parties have an interest in being committed to each other for a longer-term period, which essentially lasts between 15 to 20 years in a management agreement. HMAs are comprehensive contracts that require careful drafting from both commercial and legal perspectives. When the HMA is drafted, lawyers, business development executives, CEOs, and the Chief of Finance usually meet with the owner's representatives to negotiate each term of the HMA. This process may take days, weeks, months, or even sometimes a year, depending on how comprehensive the HMA is and the requests of each party in the agreement. When we talk about HMAs, we also discuss their application within each business in the hospitality industry, such as hotels. Hotels are often considered a more complex business that encompasses everything from rooms, restaurants, clubs, and outlets to sometimes barber shops, spas, and other facilities leased out to another brand or owner. Therefore, the examples we demonstrate can be also reflected on another businesses such as restaurants, bars or club within the industry. Back again, If the owner and the operator can negotiate the terms and conditions of the contracts in detail over a certain long period, then why should they need to resort to the courts when failing to meet some of the terms or when one of the parties is not able to fulfil its obligations towards the other?

In 2021, InterContinental Hotels Group (IHG), a major multinational hospitality operator, initiated legal proceedings in the Supreme Court of New South Wales, Australia against a hotel owner who had disposed of property subject to a hotel management agreement (HMA) with IHG, breaching contractual obligations. The court found the owner in breach for transferring hotel land without IHG's consent, awarding damages of approximately AUD 11 million plus costs to IHG. This landmark decision emphasizes the legal consequences of breaching HMAs and sets a precedent for future cases involving similar circumstances. However, disputes over damages assessment and mitigation strategy.[17]

Although the case is summarized in one paragraph, it is clear that this case has taken a long time in court to reach such a decision. Such a breach could have been mediated or negotiated if the parties were willing to do so and their interest was to continue the relationship. However, what we conclude here is that the IHG brand now has a legal case, and its name is now over the courts in Australia. The case can be found on the legal channels, and the same goes for the owner. This is what I always mention here: what is the need for a dispute if we can solve problems amicably? Especially in this case, it was only about sending an email and getting IHG's consent. It could have been resolved by saying, "We apologize for the inconvenience caused. We knew this was not correct, but we needed the money and were afraid the purchaser would withdraw."

1.2 Litigation

HMA's will not contain the same general covenants found in a commercial property lease agreement, but the underlying substantive law (which is often state-specific) will form the basis for the form and structure of such a landlord or owner future hotel management agreement. The typical hotel management agreement is substantially more complex and detailed and depends on the property's location, nature, and finances as it governs the relationship between the hotel owner and the hotel operator or, as many have historically argued, the manager. This unique type of contract is often a creature of the luxury and upper-upscale hotel management arena (reflecting the financial complexities of such high-quality physical product).

The hotel industry in the United States has been especially bombarded with litigation, and the nature and extent of such actions in many instances have involved disputes regarding hotel management, franchise,

---

[17] IHG Hotels Management (Australia) Pty Ltd v Green Garden Development No 1 Pty Ltd [2021] NSWSC 1310 ("IHG Case")

and related agreements such as licensing and branding pacts. Hotel management agreements are central to this phenomenon. This Multi-Jurisdictional Survey will examine disputes in the context of owner-operator hotel management agreements and their intersection with other aspects of hospitality law such as the selection of the corporate governance structure, franchise, trademarks, and service marks. A review of the most significant cases will be presented. Many different types of disputes are unique to hotel management agreement contracts, and as a general proposition, it can be stated that they are similar in both scope and breadth to other real estate owner-operator-lessee agreements and in innovation and development of new concepts.

1.3 *Arbitration*

Arbitration was widely considered a solution for long-winded and expensive disputes resolved through the conventional courts. The "Convention on the Recognition and Enforcement of Foreign Arbitral Awards," commonly known as the New York Convention, signed in 1958, is one of the most successful international treaties, yet its importance is often under appreciated outside the realm of international law. This treaty, in a concise 16 articles, obligates national governments to recognize written agreements to arbitrate disputes and to enforce the awards resulting from these arbitrations. It also provides a limited set of grounds on which enforcement may be refused.

Although it is now generally accepted that the increased use of arbitration has brought with it many of the same problems that hinder commercial courts, arbitration still holds a degree of attraction. It is said that the language in an arbitral award is easier to understand and more accessible to a wider audience than the language used by a judge in a common law dispute. It is quicker and, generally, cheaper. In addition, the courts have shown a renewed appreciation for arbitration and will generally strive to maintain the integrity of the arbitral process while ensuring that the arbitrators do not exceed their powers. It is not surprising, therefore, that arbitration remains an exclusive club whose members shake off much of the flotsam that has attached itself to the conventional court system in recent years.

Arbitration can address various disputes in the hotel industry, particularly those of significant severity suitable as an alternative to expert determination or judicial resolution. These disputes can involve the scope and validity of a significant management or franchise agreements, claims of wrongful termination of these significant agreement, owner claims of mismanagement by the management company, owner-contractor disputes regarding the construction of a new hotel, interpretation of collective bargaining agreements, and franchisor claims that the hotel fails to comply with mandated standards.

There are numerous advantages to arbitration for resolving disputes. Both parties usually agree on the arbitrator, ensuring impartiality and fairness. Disputes are typically resolved sooner since arbitration dates can be obtained faster than court dates. Arbitration is generally less expensive due to lower preparation costs and relaxed rules of evidence. Additionally, arbitration is a private procedure, allowing for confidentiality. Binding arbitration offers finality, with limited opportunities for appeal. It is also suitable for international disputes where parties do not want to submit to a foreign court's jurisdiction.

However, arbitration has some drawbacks. Binding arbitration means giving up the right to appeal, leaving no opportunity to correct perceived errors. Arbitration only occurs if all parties in a lawsuit agree to forgo court. Frequently, the contract underlying the parties' transactions contains a mandatory arbitration provision. If the relationship between the parties deteriorates, there may be regret about having waived the right to court proceedings. This was the situation in two recent hospitality cases.

The first case involved Fox Valley Hospitality (FVH), which operates a DoubleTree Hotel in Appleton, Wisconsin, in USA. FVH contracted with Hotel Connections, a company that manages airline crew logistics.

DoubleTree agreed to provide hotel rooms at a reduced rate to pilots and other airline personnel. Hotel Connections allegedly delayed payments, prompting FVH to sue in a Wisconsin court. However, the parties' contract included a clause mandating arbitration of disputes in Delaware, far from Wisconsin. Hotel Connections sought to dismiss the case and compel arbitration in Delaware. The judge upheld the arbitration clause and dismissed the court case.

In the second lawsuit, the plaintiffs included 90 Choice Hotels International franchisees from various locations across the country. They filed complaints against the franchisor, Choice Hotels. The plaintiffs alleged that Choice Hotels required franchisees to pay inflated prices to third-party vendors, discriminated against hoteliers of Indian and South Asian background, imposed excessive penalties on departing franchisees, and mandated costly membership in a franchise association that plaintiffs found unhelpful.

The franchise contract required arbitration of disputes in Maryland, where Choice Hotels' headquarters is located. The contract also stipulated that the losing party must pay the prevailing party's attorney's fees and all arbitration costs, which can be quite expensive. Additionally, the contract prohibited class action arbitration. The 90 franchisees asked the court to declare these clauses void due to gross unfairness. They claimed that when they first affiliated with Choice Hotels, the contract was presented as a take-it-or-leave-it agreement, with no opportunity to negotiate the terms.

The court refused to invalidate the provisions and instead dismissed the court case, ordering arbitration. The judge reasoned that the plaintiffs, as business entities, were expected to be sophisticated in business dealings. The court noted that all plaintiffs "could have walked away before signing" and that none were forced to brand their hotel properties with a Choice mark.

1.4 Mediation

In the context of the hospitality industry, mediation gives private parties a forum for developing creative solutions and preserving valuable commercial relationships without being afforded by traditional litigation or the newly adopted mechanism Arbitration. It offers an opportunity for speedy resolution, reduced litigation costs, the avoidance of procedural delays and the opportunity for the parties to appeal failing to reach a clear settlement.

Mediation is consensual, so no one feels 'summoned to appear in court.' It brings the parties together before their relationship is destroyed. The mediator, chosen for their relevant experience, knows the industry and has specific expertise related to the matter. The mediator is acceptable to both parties, and the parties contribute to the process that results in a mutually acceptable resolution. The cost of a mediator is not exorbitant, and lawyer involvement is minimal in most cases. Scheduling is flexible and up to the parties.

Although the mediation process may take longer than the arbitration and litigation, however through the mediation process parties usually reach to some points that are mostly result from the brainstorming sessions either jointly or separately conducted by the mediators at each stage of the mediation process. These ideas are most probably a way towards resolving the challenges amicably to strengthen the relationship between parties, whereas no binding award is issued until the agreement is memorialized in a written agreement executed by both parties, other evidences are left to the mediator, who is not constrained by formal rules of pre-trial discovery or rules governing evidence admission during a trial. Each party will reveal its position during the process.

A Hotel Mediation Case Example, for years, a hotel used a particular vendor for linen services. Then, a new driver was assigned to the account and quickly became verbally abusive to the hotel receiving clerk and her manager. Despite repeated complaints, the vendor management did not respond. The hotel filed notice to cancel the contract, but the vendor refused to meet with hotel management and instead filed a lawsuit for damages from the cancelled contract. Because the claimed damages fell within state-mandated amounts requiring mediation before a trial, the case was directed to mediation.

Within two hours of discussions managed by an independent mediator, the vendor dismissed the case. Both parties left the mediation relieved and reaffirmed their value to each other. The vendor apologized to the hotel staff, reinstated the contract, and dismissed the abusive driver. Both parties preserved an important relationship.

This case, though involving a relatively small sum, highlights the importance of mediation in limiting legal costs, business disruption, and management time dedicated to the issue, as well as the unpredictability of a court decision. Whether it's a simple vendor dispute, an employee/employer conflict, or a larger issue like a management contract challenge, mediation should be considered the first course of action to prevent escalation.

CHAPTER SIX

UNDERSTANDING MEDIATION

"The biggest communication problem is we do not listen to understand. We listen to reply." — Stephen R. Covey

CHAPTER SIX: UNDERSTANDING MEDIATION

1. The Rise of Mediation.

Mediation was practiced in the Middle East hundreds of years ago. In reality, the concept of deferring to a neutral and objective third party for a decision on a disagreement is well rooted in Arabic/Islamic traditions. For example, one of the most well-known legends from Prophet Muhammad's early childhood is that he was chosen by contending tribes to settle a disagreement over the restoration of the Ka'aba. Muhammad demonstrated via his live example that he was the most genuine and honest person of his day. He was a destitute orphan who began trading with his uncle, but he quickly rose to prominence and respect as a result of his honest and fair dealings with everyone. Every Makkan, affluent or poor, recognized him as As-Sadiq (the Truthful) and Al-Amin (the Trustworthy). When Muhammad was a young man, the Ka'bah was reconstructed. A debate erupted among Makkah's numerous tribes over who should have the honor of placing the Black Stone in its proper location in the Ka'bah. They agreed that the first person to enter the Ka'bah the next morning would resolve the matter. Muhammad was the first to enter that morning, and when the people saw him, they were relieved that Al-Amin and As-Sadiq had arrived and would make the decision. He placed the Black Stone on a cloth so that each tribe could grasp it and assist hoist the stone, which he then deposited in place.

The Prophet reconciled the disputing parties by proposing a unique solution that benefitted both. Islamic Law (Shari'a) promotes the notion of an impartial mediator through the practice of Al Wasata. This is fairly similar to current mediation approaches. Al Wasata is the practice of one or more people participating in a disagreement, whether at the request of one or both sides or on their own initiative. The impartial mediator seeks to mediate the issue by providing solutions to the parties, who then have the option of accepting or rejecting the proposals.

Furthermore, the Middle Eastern rituals of sulh (settlement) and musalaha (reconciliation) are forms of conflict resolution unique to the region. The sulh ritual, which originated in tribal and village settings, is an institutionalized method of dispute resolution. Sulh is a type of contract that is legally binding at both the individual and communal levels. Sulh produces two sorts of results: complete sulh and partial or conditional sulh. The former resolves all forms of dispute between the two parties, whereas the latter resolves the conflict between the two parties in accordance with the terms agreed upon during the settlement process. Sulh rituals often conclude with a public musalaha (reconciliation) ceremony. Today, sulh and musalaha rites are practiced in rural regions of Lebanon, including the Bekaa Valley, the Hermel area in eastern Lebanon, and the Akkar region in northern Lebanon. The government of Jordan officially acknowledges sulh and musalaha as a legally valid Bedouin tribal practice. This history and methodology continue to have an impact on Middle Eastern mediation techniques.

Mediation has long been used to settle conflicts between tribes and adjacent nations in the Middle East, and it is still the favored option today. Modern Islamic law emphasizes conflict resolution through direct settlement or third-party involvement. Examples like this abound throughout the Muslim world. In Jordan, the Law on Mediation for the Resolution of Civil Disputes was passed in 2006. According to Article 3 of this law, the presiding court may refer the issue to a mediating judge or a private mediator for peaceful resolution with the parties' consent or at their request. In the United Arab Emirates, the Emirate of Dubai built a Mediation Center by virtue of Dubai's Law No. 16 of 2009. The Dubai International Financial Centre Courts (DIFC courts) incorporate mediation into some proceedings, and its relevant Rules emphasize the benefits of using mediation as an alternate method of addressing specific situations. Additionally, the DIFC-LCIA Arbitration Centre, created in February 2008, provides mediation services to Centre users in accordance with the LCIA mediation procedure. In Qatar, the Qatar International Center for Conciliation and Arbitration (QICCA) was created in 2006 and approved a set of Conciliation Rules in May 2012 (the

QICCA Conciliation Rules), which were patterned on the UNCITRAL Conciliation Rules. The adoption of these rules, the establishment of these centers, and the existence of numerous mediation mechanisms through international organizations such as the International Mediation and Arbitration Center (IMAC) are all intended to encourage the use of mediation as a dispute resolution method in the Middle East today. However, unlike Middle Eastern arbitration developments, which are mostly consistent with international practices, mediation in the Middle East remains unique in a number of ways, which may serve as justification for mediation's stagnation in the region. The mediator's function is the most distinctive feature of Middle Eastern mediation. In the Arab/Islamic approach to mediation, the mediator's status and reputation, as well as the parties' respect for the mediator, are critical in reaching amicable compromise settlements. In Arab/Islamic culture, the mediator is viewed as possessing all of the answers and remedies. As a result, the mediator takes an active (i.e., fact-finding) and evaluative posture, as opposed to the Western mediator, who is neutral and acts as a facilitator, enabling the disputants to achieve a conclusion on their own.

Furthermore, whereas the Western mediator is more concerned with understanding legal procedures and structures, the Middle Eastern mediator must be more knowledgeable about the conflict's history and realities. Aside from the function and technique of the mediator, the mediator's aim differs across the two situations. Because it is critical to maintain the relationship between the parties and social harmony in the group, unlike the Western mediator, who is focused on maximising personal and group interests, the Middle Eastern mediator's goal is to restore the broken relationship between the parties and within the community. The Western mediator regards mediation as having a win/lose or win/win conclusion, but the Middle Eastern mediator regards the maintenance of societal peace as a superordinate aim.

Another significant distinction between the two techniques is that, in the West, mediation takes precedence over formal legal processes, but in the Middle East, mediation frequently occurs concurrently with a corresponding official court action. As a result, while both systems believe discretion is crucial to mediation, mediators in the Middle East may be summoned before a formal state court to testify about an agreement they have reached. It is also crucial to remember that in some countries in the Middle East, both the subject of the mediation and the mediated agreement must adhere to Shari'a. This can frequently be problematic because Shari'a prohibits riba (usury), which occurs in any commercial transaction in which one or both parties receive interest, and gharar (gambling), which has been extended by analogy to prohibit any commercial transaction in which a party's consideration is uncertain because one party may unexpectedly receive something of greater value than what they gave in exchange. These limits can be difficult to manage and limit the use of mediation as a form of dispute resolution.

Despite its strong historical and cultural basis, the Middle East has not seen an increase in the use of mediation organizations and procedures. This is most likely due to the shortage of active and trained mediators in the region, as well as a lack of trust in the mediator's capacity to make unbiased decisions. The absence of a legislative framework establishing ethics guidelines for mediators, as well as requirements for their selection and monitoring, impairs the problem. Because both history and current trends in the area promote the use of mediation, resolving these concerns is likely to result in an increase in the use of mediation in the Middle East.

2. Mediation In the Modern Era.

So what is the modern mediation? Modern mediation involves a neutral third party intervening between conflicting parties to promote reconciliation, settlement, or compromise. While a dictionary definition provides a basic understanding, to fully appreciate mediation's nature, we must consider its characteristics, advantages, and disadvantages in various contexts. In everyday life, mediation often occurs informally, with neighbours, friends, and family members frequently helping conflicting parties resolve disputes personally.

Indeed, most disputes are resolved directly by the parties involved, often after seeking advice and counsel from others. These informal mediators play a crucial role in facilitating communication and understanding, which can lead to resolution.

In more formal settings, mediation is a structured process where a professional mediator assists parties in resolving their disputes. This formal mediation is particularly relevant in industries where disputes are common, such as hospitality. Disputes in the hospitality industry are frequent due to several factors. First, many disputes arise from miscommunication or misunderstandings rather than the actual issues being addressed, particularly in hospitality, where customer service interactions are frequent and complex. Second, economic fluctuations leading to falling demand and increasing overcapacity create stress and disagreements among stakeholders. Third, the hospitality industry has unique operational features that make forecasting difficult and less precise, leading to disputes over resource allocation and service delivery. Lastly, hedging and risk-sharing mechanisms may not be as effective in hospitality due to its unpredictable nature, causing disagreements on financial and operational matters.

Despite these challenges, mediation offers several advantages. It is generally less expensive than litigation, saving both time and money. Moreover, mediation provides flexible solutions tailored to the parties' needs, focusing on collaborative solutions that can help preserve business relationships. However, there are also disadvantages to mediation. Mediation agreements are not legally binding unless formalized in a contract, and successful mediation depends heavily on the willingness of both parties to cooperate. Additionally, the outcome can significantly depend on the mediator's skill and experience.

In conclusion, mediation, whether informal or formal, plays a vital role in resolving disputes in the modern era. Its relevance is particularly pronounced in industries like hospitality, where unique challenges make disputes more likely. By understanding the characteristics, advantages, and disadvantages of mediation, businesses and individuals can navigate conflicts more effectively, promoting resolution and maintaining relationships.

3. Challenges and Limitations of Mediation in the Hospitality Industry.

The mediation model outlined highlights factors that may negatively impact hospitality workplace mediation. If not managed correctly, mediation can strain existing strategies. It is recommended that individuals be informed of the mediation policy and process rather than merely being 'invited' to mediate. A common complaint among hospitality employees is the lack of formal channels for complaint resolution, which can escalate subtle workplace conflicts into more pronounced and destructive aggression. In cases of disputes, tort law often mandates mediation as a policy. A study involved interviews with 24 senior tort lawyers to examine the use of mediation in medical negligence cases. The data analysis revealed that the participants appreciated mediation as a case management tool that helped clients avoid the stress of litigation. Some lawyers specifically mentioned the Australian Civil Procedure Act 2010 (Vic) as encouraging mediation. However, these experienced lawyers often took control of the mediation process, protecting their clients from the legal system but also dominating the proceedings. Most participants discouraged their clients from speaking and prevented emotional interactions and dialogue with the party at fault. The research found that the approach used by senior tort lawyers resembled an evaluative or settlement-focused style of mediation. This approach limited the full potential of mediation and reduced opportunities for the parties to express themselves. The authors suggested that better education for tort lawyers on the benefits of mediation could better address the non-legal and emotional needs of those involved in disputes.[18]

---
[18] T. Popa and K. Douglas, "Best for the Protagonists Involved: Views from Senior Tort Lawyers on the Value of Mediation in Victorian Medical Negligence Disputes," Monash University Law Review, vol. 45, no. 2, p. 333, Jan. 2020

Challenges in mediation often stem from parties' reluctance to consent to the process. They may prefer arbitration, believing it offers an advantage by knowing the other party's case in advance, compared to the uncertainty and tension of mediation. This preference can be addressed through enhanced dialogue and careful listening. It's crucial for mediation planners to communicate actively with participants before the mediation begins. This pre-mediation communication allows parties to express their concerns and helps build trust, which is essential for a successful mediation. Research shows that failing to consult with parties beforehand can delay the mediation process.

For instance, when a customer of a hospitality establishment has a complaint, he should attempt to resolve the complaint at the lowest possible level. Most reasonable people avoid confrontation unless the issue is very serious. The customer with a simple complaint involving a hotel should have a conversation with the supervisor on duty or the duty manager. Hopefully, review by the supervisor can lead to a resolution with the customer deciding to stay at the same establishment next time or perhaps look at other horizons. Depending on how the supervisor handles the complaint, this will be the first level of evidence a judge or jury will consider in deciding the liability of and the profits accruing to the lodging proprietor. But what if the supervisor's resolution annoys the customer? What if the customer leaves the establishment in a less than joyful state of mind with thoughts of revenge against management? This needs a thorough understanding of the consequences, and the management must be prepared for the implications that may occur due to the unsatisfied customer.

Examples of Mediation in the Hospitality Industry.

Hotel Owner and Franchisee Dispute:

Consider a dispute between a hotel owner and a franchisee. The owner might feel that the hotel's management practices, such as inconsistent service standards or poor maintenance, are affecting their profitability. To verify these concerns, the franchisee can present data such as customer complaints, online reviews, occupancy rates, and maintenance logs that demonstrate otherwise, which may show the hotel owner that the franchisee is following the terms and conditions of the agreement adequately.

For instance, during pre-mediation talks, the franchisee might reveal specific incidents where the management avoided guest complaints, that was going to impact their revenue and reputation. They might present evidence such as negative online reviews mentioning unclean rooms or broken amenities, which can be linked to a drop in bookings and revenue and how the management sorted them in a professional way.

The mediator can then use this information to guide the mediation process, ensuring that both parties come to the table with a clearer understanding of the issues. This helps reduce the uncertainty and tension associated with mediation. By addressing the franchisee's points upfront, the mediator can help the hotel owner see the impact of their practices and reveal these points and clarify them to the owner, by using some mediation techniques that can help address the points clearly and relieving the tensions between the owner and the franchisee.

Restaurant Operator and Hotel Manager Conflict:

In another example, a conflict might arise between a restaurant operator and a hotel management over shared space usage. The restaurant operator may feel that the hotel's events, such as conferences or weddings, are disrupting their business by occupying common areas or creating noise that drives away diners. Early communication in the mediation process can bring these grievances to light.

For instance, during pre-mediation discussions, the restaurant operator might share specific dates when hotel events caused a significant drop in their business. The mediator can then facilitate a conversation where both parties discuss scheduling and space management, allowing them to address these operational issues constructively. They might agree on better communication about event schedules or soundproofing measures to minimize disruption, leading to a more harmonious relationship.

Condo-Hotel Developer and Unit Purchasers:

A condo-hotel developer and unit purchasers may be at odds over property maintenance issues. The purchasers might feel that the developer is not fulfilling their obligations, leading to deteriorating property conditions. Through active pre-mediation communication, the mediator can uncover these concerns and assure both sides that their issues will be addressed.

For example, unit purchasers might share detailed accounts of maintenance failures, such as broken amenities or delayed repairs, which affect their living experience and investment value. The mediator can then guide the discussion towards finding practical solutions, like setting up a more transparent maintenance schedule or improving the communication channel for reporting and addressing issues.

Maintaining Voluntary Participation:

Mediation should be part of the agreement as to ADR to maintain its integrity. Once consent to mediate is achieved, the mediator should facilitate the parties to reach a settlement rather than adhering to the contract terms and conditions such as in arbitration or litigation and reinforce them without discussion. This approach builds on the principle of fostering a continuous, cooperative and effective business relationship rather than ending or terminating it.

By intensifying dialogue and listening carefully to the parties, mediation planners can overcome initial reluctance. Effective mediation in the hospitality industry relies on understanding and addressing the parties' concerns early. This proactive approach ensures that the mediation process is smooth, , and based on mutual trust and understanding, ultimately leading to resolutions that preserve relationships and enhance operational efficiency.

4. Benefits of Mediation in the Hospitality Industry.

Multiple mediation providers have expertise in the hospitality industry. Whether your claim is with or against a cruise line or tour operator, hotel or facility staff, a claim arising from a timeshare, or against a construction firm, there are hundreds of esteemed professionals available to assist in a resolution being reached. For example, the American Arbitration Association has of approximately 7,500 of the best arbitrators and mediators from more than 45 nations[19]. Additionally, several global providers specialize in particular issues that occur in many disputes, including crop insurance and loss adjusting. =

The hospitality industry is a multi-faceted niche that requires focusing on different aspects, including the satisfaction, expectations, and complaints of its guests and customers. In fact, the average hospitality business hears from only 10% of its dissatisfied customers, while 90% of customers will neither voluntarily do business with an establishment after just one adverse encounter nor visit the establishment as a guest again. The key to aiding in resolving a broad range of disputes in the hospitality industry, such as guest disputes or contracting disputes, is mediation. Mediation can lead to a range of benefits for both parties,

---

19 The AAA Statement of Ethical Principles provides guidance on ethical conduct within the realm of arbitration and mediation. Established by the American Arbitration Association (AAA), an organization comprising over 8,000 members, including approximately 7,500 arbitrators and mediators, these principles outline fundamental values and standards upheld by practitioners in the field.

For more information, refer to: AAA Statement of Ethical Principles.

and in some cases may satisfy the interests of both the claimant and the respondent, saving clients time, money, and stress. For example, addressing complaints from guests about hotel room conditions can pose significant challenges for service providers. Often, verifying the reported faults proves difficult for managers. Typically, managers opt to transfer the guest to another room or provide an upgrade to prevent future grievances, sometimes labelling the guest as a "trouble maker" based on past experiences with the same guest or during the same stay. The varied perceptions among hospitality personnel regarding such guests often lead to attempts to avoid their opinions altogether.

Based on personal observations and experiences, it's evident that many managers recognize underlying infrastructure issues of the establishment as the root cause of recurring problems, which they are unable to address directly. Consequently, these unresolved structural deficiencies persist, potentially leading to disputes, particularly when problems escalate and impact guest health.

GMs commonly anticipate disputes arising from these persistent infrastructure issues, despite the tendency of both owners and operators to overlook them. While management is expected to resolve such issues, frustrations may arise during mediation sessions, where GMs may confidentially pinpoint infrastructure deficiencies as contributing factors. This feedback can prompt subsequent action from the hotel operator or corporate office, leading to immediate resolutions with the owner. Ultimately, such interventions not only help resolve disputes but also enable GMs and staff members to focus on revenue generation rather than problem-solving. Consequently, it may be helpful for the disputing parties' resort to utilizing outside mediators or neutrals as expert witnesses to resolve these disputed claims.

5. Mediation vs. Litigation: A Comparison.

In addition to time and cost, humility and fairness also play a role in the mediation process. Parties approach mediation proceedings for many reasons, says Chris Moore in his book The Mediation Process: Practical Strategies for Resolving Conflict "mediation can be described as an ADR method were an acceptable, uninvolved and unbiased third party intervenes in a negotiation or conflict. The third party is usually known as mediator, which has only a limited access to information and no official decision-making power " [20] .Thus, parties may approach mediation sessions with a degree of humility and willingness to negotiate openly. This is not the case in litigation. In litigation, a party may feel unduly defensive or threatened, thus creating a hindrance to the fair and balanced resolution of the dispute. Consequently, this difference in approach further fuels the litigation machine and is proof of the many advantages mediation has to offer. Not only is mediation fair, quick, and cost-efficient, but it also helps parties find a resolution that they are responsible for.

The mediation process is typically shorter than the litigation process. Business professionals like to get the disputes behind them and continue their forward motion. Mediation allows businesspeople to solve the problem and move on. The litigation process can be a distraction and requires extensive information gathering. "It's okay for management to manage, but if all it has to do is prepare for and testify in litigation, its focus inevitably shifts from the operation of the business to the litigation of disputes with customers, suppliers, employees, or financial backers. It is no coincidence that many businesses that find themselves in litigation do not thrive." "Management should be free to manage the business in the normal course rather than getting laid low by litigation." Litigation carries inherent risks and uncertainties, especially in multicultural environments such as the UAE, Qatar, and Saudi Arabia. In these regions, cultural differences significantly impact organizational disputes. Organizational policies and regulations often overlook these cultural nuances, adhering instead to standardized protocols set by hotel operators or management.

For instance, cultural differences can shape how employees perceive employer actions during challenges

---
20 C. W. Moore, The Mediation Process: Practical Strategies for Resolving Conflict, 3rd ed. San Francisco: Jossey-Bass, 2003.

like the COVID-19 pandemic. Measures such as salary reductions or unpaid leave might be viewed differently across various cultural backgrounds, potentially leading to disputes. In Dubai, for example, employment disputes frequently stem from pandemic-related measures such as salary cuts, unpaid leave, and company restructuring. These disputes are further impaired by cultural differences that influence employee perceptions and reactions to these measures. For instance, employees from certain cultural backgrounds might view salary reductions as a breach of trust, while others might see unpaid leave as a sign of job insecurity. Additionally, the rapid implementation of these measures without adequate communication can lead to misunderstandings and heightened tensions.

Furthermore, disputes can also arise from varying interpretations of contract terms, differences in work ethics, and expectations influenced by cultural norms. For example, in some cultures, loyalty to an employer might discourage employees from questioning decisions, in others, employees might be more likely to challenge actions they see as unfair or unjust. These cultural factors contribute to the complexity of managing employment disputes in a diverse environment like Dubai. You may need to know why we have taken UAE as example, employment disputes in onshore Dubai, except the Dubai International Financial Centre (DIFC) and other Dubai freezones such as Jebel Ali Freezone (JAFZA) Dubai Multi Commodities Centre (DMCC) and others, are resolved according to the UAE Federal Decree-Law No. (33) of 2021. This law outlines the dispute resolution process for employment-related issues, ensuring that all disputes are handled in accordance with federal regulations. Thus although that most of these jurisdictions are located on the land of Dubai, however each of them has its own laws and regulations that needs to be taken in consideration in terms of litigation.

In cases where internal resolution of disputes with employees proves unsuccessful, in Dubai onshore companies known as (Mainland Companies) the employee is required to lodge a complaint either with the Ministry of HRs and Emiratisation (MoHRE) Representatives from either MoHRE or the relevant free trade labour department then endeavour to mediate the matter before initiating formal court proceedings. The conciliation process varies across entities, with examples like the DMCC offering mediation services using trained mediators. Should the dispute remain unresolved two weeks after filing the initial complaint, the Labor Law mandates MoHRE or the relevant labour department to refer the matter to the Labor Courts through a 'transfer letter', allowing the employee to proceed with their claim within six months. Subsequently, the Labor Courts schedule appointments and require written pleadings, often necessitating legal counsel due to limited rights of hearing and the complexity of claims. After evaluating the written submissions, the court delivers its judgment orally and in writing, with the option for either party to appeal. Despite the legal merits, the costs and time associated with defending claims to judgment often influence an employer's response. Such costs typically encompass court filing fees, legal expenses, and expert fees, the burden of which varies depending on the outcome and nature of the claim.[21]

Consequently, claims are commonly filed pertaining to unpaid or reduced salaries, breaches of contract, unlawful dismissals, challenges related to company restructures, and instances where employees breach restrictive covenants by affiliating with competitors, settling during mediation allows the parties to control the outcome. This fact alone is extremely important to most businesses, cost is another factor to consider. Mediation is considerably less expensive than litigation. For example, the discovery process, exchanging documents between the parties, the taking of testimony and experts, and the filing of legal briefs, motions, and cross motions can all cost a substantial amount of money. The average litigation now takes 1-3 years to resolve – what other options are there? What does one do if they want a dispute resolved in a matter of weeks or months, not years?

---

[21] Employment Disputes in Dubai and the DIFC Courts," published on July 29, 2020, at 4:24 pm. Pinsent Masons is the law firm associated with Out-Law. pinsentmasons.com/out-law/guides/employment-disputes-dubai-difc.

6. The Role of Mediators in Resolving Disputes.

Mediation is one of the most powerful tools used to minimize the impact that a conflict may have on the hospitality establishment and one of the easiest procedures to implement. When various forms of mediation are brought into play, the parties are given the opportunity to interact in a neutral setting in the presence of a skilled mediator. Mediators are individuals who, by virtue of their life and work experiences, as well as through training and practice, are able to facilitate the transformation of conflict. They are, in essence, 'neutral' parties. This role of being neutral is of essence and direction, as it forces mediators to abstain from decisions that would have been made by the disagreeing parties. To accomplish this stance, a mediator cannot know the parties. This is because relationships are built on similarities; it is through the understanding of the basics of ease that natural connections that ultimately develop an attorney, whereas a judge rules impartially. An efficient mediator should possess the talent to facilitate an understanding between both opposing parties. Moreover, it is also the role of mediators to manage and settle the differences amicably without bias. Even though in contentious proceedings there may be arbitrators to direct the daily progress of the case, in various settings the actual disputes will be resolved informally among the mediators themselves, who operate under the direction of a senior partner.

Conflict, particularly in the unique environment of the hotel industry, is inevitable. It is how conflicts are resolved that governs how the hotel's business will be affected. As stated earlier, opting to resolve disputes in the courtroom causes business relationships to sever. In a time when the global economic climate is unstable, the role of the mediator has thus become essential in reframing and resolving mediation. By dissecting the mediation process and by examining these principles' application to disputes in the hospitality industry, hoteliers, in formulating their plans for resolving disputes, can hopefully opt for the less adversarial option of mediation, which would be a step in the right direction in facilitating continued harmonious business relationships.

7. Mediation Training and Certification for Hospitality Professionals.

Mediation Training Program. With the growing demand for effective dispute resolution in the hospitality industry, the need for certified mediators from reputable institutions like the International Mediation Institute (IMI) is paramount. IMI-certified mediators are equipped with diverse skills in various commercial aspects and undergo training through a network of centres worldwide. Recognizing the unique challenges faced by the hospitality sector, it is imperative to establish a dedicated category for hospitality mediation within reputable institutions like IMI or the AMC Institute, as well as organizations such as the American Hotel & Lodging Association (AH&LA), ASAE & The Centre for Association Leadership, Association of Collegiate Conference and Events Directors-International (ACCED-I), and Association of Destination Management Executives International (ADME International).

Collaborating with these industry associations can ensure that the training programs for hospitality mediators meet the specific needs and standards of the hospitality sector. For example, the AMC Institute, as an international nonprofit trade association, comprises companies that provide association management and professional services. By accrediting their certification programs for hospitality mediators through IMI, these companies can offer specialized training to professionals serving volunteer-governed organizations and for-profit companies in the hospitality industry.

Similarly, organizations like AH&LA, ASAE & The Centre, ACCED-I, and ADME International play crucial roles in representing and supporting professionals in various aspects of the hospitality sector, including lodging, association management, events planning, and destination management. By accrediting their certification programs for hospitality mediators through IMI, these associations can ensure that their members have access to high-quality training and certification that aligns with international mediation standards.

Establishing a specialized category for hospitality mediation within IMI or these industry associations requires a strategic approach. This includes conducting industry needs assessments, forging collaborative partnerships, developing tailored curricula, establishing robust training delivery mechanisms, defining clear certification criteria, promoting awareness, and continuously improving the program based on feedback and emerging trends.

In conclusion, through strategic collaboration with industry associations and reputable institutions like IMI, the establishment of a specialized certification program for hospitality mediators can address the growing demand for proficient dispute resolution expertise within the hospitality sector. This initiative ensures that professionals in the hospitality industry have access to specialized training and certification that meets international standards and reflects the unique challenges and dynamics of the hospitality sector.

8. Mediation Policies and Procedures in the Hospitality Industry.

In the dynamic environment of the hospitality industry, conflicts are inevitable due to the diverse range of stakeholders involved, including guests, staff, management, and external partners. These conflicts can arise from various sources such as misunderstandings, differing expectations, cultural differences, or resource allocation issues. Left unaddressed, conflicts can escalate, negatively impacting guest satisfaction, employee morale, and overall organizational performance. Recognizing the potential consequences of unresolved conflicts, forward-thinking hospitality establishments prioritize the development of mediation policies and procedures. These policies serve as proactive measures aimed at effectively managing conflicts before they escalate into larger issues. By implementing structured mediation processes, organizations can facilitate constructive dialogue, identify underlying issues, and work towards mutually acceptable resolutions.

For instance, let's consider the case of Deb and Linda, two experienced employees within a hospitality establishment. Deb and Linda are well-known for their natural ability to navigate conflicts and resolve disputes among colleagues and guests. Instead of allowing conflicts to fester and potentially disrupt operations, Deb and Linda proactively intervene, using their communication skills and conflict resolution techniques to address issues as they arise.

Mediation policies and procedures in the hospitality industry encompass a range of strategies tailored to address the unique challenges faced by the sector. These strategies may include establishing clear communication channels for reporting conflicts, designating trained mediators or conflict resolution specialists, and providing ongoing training and support for staff members involved in conflict resolution roles. Furthermore, effective mediation policies emphasize the importance of early intervention to prevent conflicts from escalating. By addressing issues promptly and impartially, organizations can minimize disruptions to operations and maintain positive relationships with guests, employees, and other stakeholders.

In addition to conflict resolution, mediation policies in the hospitality industry also focus on proactive measures to prevent conflicts from occurring in the first place. This may involve fostering a culture of open communication, promoting teamwork and collaboration, and addressing underlying issues that contribute to conflict, such as ineffective leadership or inadequate resources.

Overall, mediation policies and procedures play a vital role in promoting a positive organizational culture and ensuring the smooth operation of hospitality establishments. By proactively managing conflicts and promoting constructive dialogue, organizations can enhance guest experiences, improve employee morale, and ultimately achieve long-term success in the competitive hospitality industry.

9. Mediation Ethics and Professional Standards.

Often, and for a variety of reasons, individuals involved in a dispute, and who may have agreed to mediated attempts to resolve their dispute, will reverse course and challenge the morals or ethics of the mediator and their fair administration of the process. Resolving to continue with mediation or suspend the process is a complex and, hopefully, rare decision the mediator will need to make. There are a few broad sets of relationship issues involving lawyers and other trained participants in the mediation environment. In general, the circulating ethical principles point towards neutrality, limits to confidentiality, and fairness. For example, the standards suggest that when using a mediator whose primary language is not that of the disputant, or when there is fear or insecurity, mediators should inform parties to use the services of an interpreter if necessary.

The mediator, as a relatively neutral third party, is a role model in terms of ethics, professional standards, and conduct when they are involved in the process of mediation. As practitioners, mediators are expected to uphold ethical guidelines and professional standards of conduct, beginning with the key essential qualifications of confidentiality and neutrality. Mediators need to maintain the confidentiality of the process by not discussing what happens at the session with non-participants or releasing information unless required by law. In addition, the mediator must, in spirit and in action, create and maintain a neutral environment that allows the parties sufficient opportunity to present their own interests towards an eventual agreement outcome.

In the case of Vitakis-Valchine v. Valchine, the court held that, according to Florida law, contracts or settlements cannot be invalidated based on duress or coercion unless the improper influence originates from one of the contracting parties. However, the record supported the finding that neither party nor their attorneys were involved in any duress or coercion. The case involved a mediated settlement agreement reached during court-ordered mediation, where the wife alleged misconduct by the mediator, including coercion and improper influence. The court ruled that mediator misconduct could be grounds for not enforcing a settlement agreement. The court emphasized the importance of adherence to proper mediation procedures and ethics, as mediators are considered agents of the court during court-ordered mediation. While no findings were made regarding the alleged misconduct, the case was remanded for further investigation into the mediator's actions and their impact on the settlement agreement.[22]

Accordingly, the mediator code of ethics, as outlined in various sources such as the American Bar Association (ABA) Guidelines for Litigation Conduct and Behind the Curtain: Ethics for Mediators, emphasizes several fundamental principles. These include professionalism and integrity, requiring mediators to uphold high standards of honesty, impartiality, and fairness throughout the mediation process. Confidentiality is paramount, ensuring that all discussions and information shared during mediation remain confidential to foster an environment of trust and openness. Neutrality and impartiality are also central, necessitating that mediators remain unbiased and refrain from favouring any party involved. Furthermore, compliance with disciplinary rules, as outlined in state regulations like Florida's Supreme Court Rules for Certified and Court-Appointed Mediators or Alabama's Code of Ethics, is crucial. Mediators must adhere to these rules, with mechanisms in place for reviewing, investigating, and adjudicating complaints about mediator conduct to uphold accountability and maintain the integrity of the mediation process.

10. Mediation and Customer Satisfaction in the Hospitality Industry.

According to Daniel, in the UK, the Government budget deficit in 2018/19 was the lowest recorded in 17 years. The Government borrowed the equivalent of 1.2% of GDP (£24.7 billion) in 2018/19 to make up the difference between what it spent and what it received in revenues. This was the lowest since a deficit of

---

22 Vitakis-Valchine v. Valchine, 793 So. 2d 1094 (Fla. Dist. Ct. App. 2001)

0.4% in 2001/02 and down from a peak of 9.9% in 2009/10 following the financial crisis[23]. According to Hotstats financial results for UK hotels continued declining three months into 2019[24]. Like most challenges facing the industry, this can be traced to the fluctuating exchange rates because of the Brexit impasse and the lack of a trade deal between the UK and the EU. The UK has also declined its ranking over the years[25], showing a change in perception about service quality and satisfaction. While most of the challenges are economic, many are service-related issues which can only be managed by caring management, involving services geared towards handling customer dissatisfaction. Our indication of a real headache for the hotel establishment is customer satisfaction that is linked to the frequent occurrence of conflict-related issues.

The ability of the hospitality industry to manage customers' dissatisfaction and conflict is key to the commercial success of individual organizations and the industry as a whole. However, while the importance of this capability is recognized, very little empirical research is available to explore its strategic implications and methods to manage conflicts that arise. Moreover, culturally sophisticated managers often adopt their response to conflict from influential national culture values. While this may impact the satisfaction of domestic guests, international guests with different expectations remain vulnerable. For example, a hotel manager might prioritize maintaining harmony and avoiding direct confrontation in their conflict resolution approach, reflecting their cultural background. This method might satisfy local guests who value subtlety and indirect communication. However, international guests who prefer straightforward and transparent resolutions could feel their concerns are not adequately addressed, leading to increased dissatisfaction.

When managers avoid direct confrontation, it can lead to disputes by leaving issues unresolved or by giving the impression that complaints are not taken seriously. For instance, if a guest reports a problem and the manager responds indirectly, the guest might feel ignored or misunderstood. This lack of directness can escalate frustration, causing the guest to feel disrespected and prompting further complaints or negative reviews. In such scenarios, the initial conflict can grow due to perceived neglect, ultimately harming the hotel's reputation and customer relationships.

What I mostly like about the UK is the direct influence of consumer protection laws in all the service industries that serve the UK nationals and the international customer equally, UK consumer law, particularly the Consumer Rights Act 2015, ensures fair treatment and informed choices for consumers in the hospitality sector. Therefore, consumers are entitled to accurate service descriptions, competent delivery, and remedies for substandard services. For example, if a guest books a room that doesn't match the description, they can request a refund.

In the UK hospitality industry, compliance with regulations is paramount to uphold consumer rights and foster trust among guests. For instance, the Consumer Contracts Regulations 2013 ensure transparency in bookings, granting a 14-day cooling-off period. This means guests have ample time to reconsider their reservation without penalty. Furthermore, the Misleading Advertising and Unfair Trading Regulations prevent deceptive practices, safeguarding guests from being misled about services or pricing. For example, a hotel cannot advertise amenities that it does not provide.

Moreover, the UK hospitality sector benefits from ADR mechanisms, which offer swift and efficient conflict resolution. For instance, if a guest disputes a charge or service quality, ADR can facilitate a resolution without resorting to lengthy legal processes. Therefore, adherence to these regulations not only protects consumer rights but also enhances trust and loyalty within the hospitality industry. Guests feel confident

---

23 Harari, D. (2019, April 26). Brexit uncertainties and Economic Dynamics: An Insight. Economic Updates. https://commonslibrary.parliament.uk/economic-update-a-steady-start-to-2019/
24 https://www.hotstats.com/hotel-industry-trends/uk-hotels-profit-shrink-a-continuance-of-2019
25 The Fitch Wire report from October 24, 2019, highlighted the impact of declining business travel on the UK hotel sector. The challenging conditions in the UK's lodging industry, particularly affecting regional markets and the business segment, were expected to negatively influence the performance of UK-focused hoteliers in the short term. This decline was linked to broader economic uncertainties and changes in travel patterns, which were adversely affecting hotel occupancy rates and revenue per available room (RevPAR) across the UK (Fitch Ratings).

knowing that their rights are respected and upheld.

The implication of regulations, such as the Consumer Contracts Regulations and the Misleading Advertising and Unfair Trading Regulations, on ADR and mediation in the hospitality industry is significant.

Firstly, these regulations set clear standards for consumer rights and fair practices, providing a framework within which disputes may arise. When disputes occur between guests and hospitality businesses regarding bookings, services, or pricing, ADR mechanisms, including mediation, become essential for resolving conflicts efficiently and amicably.

For example, if a guest feels that they were misled about the amenities provided or encountered issues during their stay that were not adequately addressed, they may initiate a dispute. A mediation process facilitated by ADR professionals allows both parties to voice their concerns, explore potential solutions, and reach a mutually satisfactory resolution outside of court.

Moreover, compliance with these laws enhance the effectiveness of ADR and mediation by ensuring that parties enter negotiations with a clear understanding of their rights and obligations. This clarity reduces the likelihood of disputes escalating and facilitates smoother mediation processes.

In summary, UK Consumer Protection Law 2015 in the hospitality industry, not only promote consumer protection but also support the efficacy of ADR and mediation as viable avenues for resolving disputes. Compliance with these laws foster an environment where conflicts can be addressed promptly and fairly, ultimately contributing to the maintenance of trust and integrity within the industry.

On the other side, the new Consumer Protection Law in the UAE, enacted in November 2020, brings significant enhancements to consumer rights and imposes heavier penalties for infringements. Like Consumer Protection Law 2015 in the UK, it emphasizes transparency, data protection, and fair practices in the hospitality industry. For instance, it mandates disclosure of provider information and requires invoices to be in Arabic, ensuring clarity and accountability in transactions.

This legislation has implications for the hospitality sector in the UAE akin to those in the UK. It introduces provisions for E-commerce activities and protects consumer data privacy, mirroring trends in global consumer protection laws. Moreover, the inclusion of penalties, including imprisonment and fines, aims to deter misleading advertising and inadequate service provision.

The new law provides a framework for the implementation of ADR, including mediation, in the UAE hospitality sector. By addressing consumer grievances and ensuring fair resolution mechanisms, it promotes trust and integrity within the industry. Compliance with these regulations not only safeguards consumer rights but also strengthens the reputation of hospitality businesses.

In summary, the new Consumer Protection Law in the UAE, similar to regulations in the UK, underscores the importance of consumer rights and fair practices in the hospitality industry. It creates opportunities for ADR, particularly mediation, to address disputes and uphold consumer trust, contributing to the sector's growth and sustainability.

11. Mediation as a Preventive Measure for Disputes in the Hospitality Industry.

Mediation can help parties better understand the other's perspective. If implemented through an industry-wide setting, required participation or scheduled into other routes to dispute resolution, by resolving disputes early, mediation can reduce customer frustration and save additional costs for the hospitality provider, market themselves as protectors of guest services and overall provide a better customer service experience. Mediation also assists the hospitality provider in maintaining important customer relationships by encouraging cooperation, minimizing the potential for escalating the dispute and preserving rapport. Additionally, the good news from the mediation process will help maintain the professional business relationships that are considered crucial in the high-end, small setting hospitality industry. Furthermore, mediation can have a positive effect in maintaining the company's public image. Publicizing successful mediations can indicate the belief that the entity is empathetic and genuinely concerned about the public. Establishing such an image within the public domain can aid in the in-turn brand positioning within market saturated, hotel room for every budget atmosphere. By promoting this customer service differentiation, structuring service differently from the consumer perceptive rather than using a business-to-business promotional tactic.

Mediation is a preventive measure for resolving disputes that arise within the hospitality industry. Hospitality environments are ripe for potential disputes due to consumer turnover, seasonal and demand/geographic shifts (e.g. conferences), and having seasonal staff as buffer when lines are long and tempers may shortly rise. Often these disputes can escalate if the guest feels the interaction was not handled properly between the two parties, leading to either no dispute with the guest leaving quietly, venting and in turn actualizing illegal actions, or withdrawing future business. Mediation has the potential to reduce multiple aspects of disputes due to a real-time, facilitated conversation focused to have a resolution where both parties feel satisfaction.

12. Mediation Effects on Burnout and Turnover in Hotel Staff.

Within the hospitality industry, the concept of "service" and "employee relations" are prerequisites for success. The efficient and effective task performance by employees to others has the potential for disruptions in service provision and thus negatively affecting workplace harmony, employee job satisfaction, and communication. The industry continues to have low job satisfaction, and employees have many grievances, with a lack of communication and interaction. Given the condition that service excellence is one of the doctrines of the hospitality industry, it is quite natural that in most cases, employee relations are built on transactions and not human interactions.

In a recent study conducted by Baquero, it investigated the significant impact of burnout (BU) and psychological distress (PD) identified as another significant factor influencing turnover intentions. Stemming from workplace demands, incivility, and aggressive leadership, psychological distress further impairs turnover intentions on the employees in the hospitality industry, particularly in the Middle East. Therefore, it's crucial to understand how these factors affect workers' well-being and organizational dynamics. The conceptual framework integrates several theories such as social cognitive theory, demands-resources theory, social exchange theory, organizational theory, and theory of emotional contagion. These theories provide a comprehensive understanding of the determinants and outcomes of burnout in the workplace.

Furthermore, the research emphasizes the adverse effects of burnout on both work-related and health-related outcomes. Burnout not only leads to a deterioration in job performance but also increases the intention to quit (ITQ) among employees. Moreover, burnout is intricately linked to factors such as lack of supervisor support, organizational pressures, and job demands exceeding resources. These factors create a challenging work environment for hospitality workers, contributing to their emotional exhaustion and diminished engagement. Furthermore, the research suggests that male workers may be more affected by burnout due to the dominance of male employees in the industry. This underscores the importance of gender-sensitive approaches in addressing burnout and promoting employee well-being.

The unfavourable working environment in the hospitality sector contributes to emotional exhaustion, depersonalization, and diminished personal accomplishment among employees. Consequently, this leads to increased turnover intentions and challenges in retaining talent within the industry.

Therefore, the research underscores the urgent need for interventions to address burnout and psychological distress in the hospitality industry, particularly in the Middle East. By prioritizing employee well-being and creating supportive work environments, organizations can mitigate turnover intentions and improve overall organizational outcomes. This is can lead us to the point that, the implementation of effective mediation practices in the Middle East hospitality sector could significantly impact the industry. Mediation can provide a constructive framework for resolving conflicts, improving communication, and fostering a positive work culture. By addressing underlying issues and promoting understanding between employers and employees, mediation can help reduce burnout and psychological distress among hospitality workers.

Furthermore, successful mediation can lead to increased employee satisfaction, higher retention rates, and improved productivity. It can also enhance the reputation of Middle Eastern hospitality businesses, making them more attractive to both customers and prospective employees.

Overall, the integration of mediation practices in the Middle East hospitality industry has the potential to create a more harmonious and sustainable work environment, benefiting both employees and organizations alike.[26]

13. Mediation and Vendor Relationships in the Hospitality Industry.

In a pre-fraud setting, the most frequently cited internal control weakness reported by external sources is the segregation of duties deficiency. This type of deficiency occurs because one person is able to initiate, approve, record, and reconcile the transaction activities. Vendors are more likely to take risks when an employee puts in a request to buy more than the company usually does, thus the more autonomy that employees are given, the more an outside party may seek to benefit from this type of request. Optimal segregation of duties, if it is possible, would mean that the individual who carries out the task of authorizing a transaction is separate and distinct from the individual who carries out the activity of reconciling such a transaction. Mediation can help expedite the process of achieving this optimal segregation of duties. In order to mediate, individuals must develop good or positive relationships with their colleagues that respect the power of one another. Colleagues with good relationships are less likely to engage in tactics that would escalate their conflicts into greater, more serious concerns.

This is targeted towards existing managers in the hospitality industry, law students, and any parties interested in understanding the relationship between managers and their vendors. "Vendors" are those individuals or entities outside an organization who provide goods or services to an organization. A common, yet serious problem for managers in the hospitality industry is vendor fraud – which can be both costly and damaging to the organization.

Let's explore deeper into the implications of UAE Federal Decree-Law No. 42/2023 to Combat Commercial Fraud, repealing Federal Law No. 19/2016, and emphasizing a comprehensive legal framework. The new law aims to protect consumers, preserve goods' integrity, and promote fair trade practices in the UAE, lets address this and demonstrate the implications of the new law in the hospitality industry and how mediation can effectively address potential issues.

Under the new law, vendors in the hospitality sector are required to comply with strict regulations aimed at combating commercial fraud. For example, if a hotel vendor is found to be selling adulterated or counterfeit goods to guests, they could face severe penalties including fines and imprisonment. Moreover, the reputational damage to the hotel could be significant, leading to loss of trust among customers and potentially impacting future business.

---

26 Baquero, A. "Hotel Employees' Burnout and Intention to Quit: The Role of Psychological Distress and Financial Well-Being in a Moderation Mediation Model," Behav. Sci., vol. 13, p. 84, 2023, doi: 10.3390/bs13020084.

In such a scenario, mediation emerges as a valuable tool for dispute resolution. Rather than resorting to lengthy and adversarial legal proceedings which may lead to the disruption of service to the guest who is the bread and butter of the hospitality industry especially if the vendor or the supplier of a unique product or service standard, mediation comes to offer a collaborative approach to resolving conflicts. A trained mediator can facilitate dialogue between the hotel and the supplier, allowing both parties to express their concerns and interests openly.

During the mediation process, the hotel may seek compensation for any harm caused to guests, such as refunds or vouchers for future stays. Meanwhile, the supplier may offer assurances of improved product quality and supply chain transparency to regain the hotel's trust.

By reaching a mutually acceptable agreement through mediation, both the hotel and the supplier can avoid the negative consequences of prolonged litigation. Moreover, the resolution fosters a positive business relationship moving forward, ensuring continued cooperation and adherence to legal standards.

Overall, mediation serves as a proactive and efficient means of addressing commercial disputes in the hospitality industry, aligning with the objectives of Federal Decree-Law No. 42/2023 to promote fair trade practices and consumer protection.

14. Mediation and Guest Complaints in the Hospitality Industry.

The business of hospitality is a service business; hotel guests, by nature, are demanding. They expect a comfortable, safe, and secure atmosphere with minimal disturbances. Conflicts are almost inevitable, and many managerial teaching programs deal with 'crisis management'. The aim of such programs is to minimize and avoid as many crises as possible. However, they rarely address the issue of how to manage a minor skirmish in its early stages before it becomes a crisis. Managers in the hotel and hospitality industry put up with a great deal when dealing with guests; otherwise, the wrath of the guest will fall on them in the form of complaints. For a manager in service professions, the first and foremost response to complaints is to win back the goodwill of the guest. This has almost always proved the most effective way to deal with the problem posed by the dissatisfied guest. Despite the vast number of research papers and articles on the issue of satisfaction, there remains little literature that examines the ways in which guest impressions can be managed and how guest complaints can be handled positively, showing that the 'respondent' is important to the organization.

In the hospitality industry, there is no secret that guest complaints are received on a day-to-day basis, regardless of the capacity of the hotel with regard to its stars or level of service. No service is perfect. The hospitality industry is among the service industries which demand face-to-face service delivery with staff who are always dealing with different types of guests, each with different behavioural styles. Dealing with guest complaints on the same or a similar subject requires employees to listen and understand the complaint negatively or positively, whether it is true or false, and decide what type of action needs to take place. It may also increase the amount of interaction time between guests and employees, as employees need to listen to complaints and react to them efficiently. Also, employees need to deal with complaints appropriately and effectively because complaints can cause bad attitudes of guests towards the hotel and could lead to a negative image of the hotel and possible financial loss. In a hotel, there are guests staying for various reasons. Some may be business travellers attending a conference, while others could be tourists exploring the city. Additionally, there might be families on vacation and individuals on solo trips. Now, let's say there's a hotel restaurant offering breakfast service. In the morning, business travellers might come down for a quick bite before heading out to their meetings. At the same time, families may gather for a leisurely breakfast together, enjoying the variety of options offered by the hotel.

Here, guests from different backgrounds and with different agendas are using the same service, the hotel restaurant, albeit for different purposes. Despite their varied needs and lengths of stay, they share communal spaces and amenities like the restaurant, pool or bars creating a diverse and dynamic environment within the hotel. Little wonder, then, that guests are frequently seen as the primary source of complaints against hotel operations. A hotel guest may complain about the perceived quality of specific features of the hotel property, the behaviour of the staff, the characteristics of another guest, or external factors that affect the guest's stay. The probability of such complaints rises as the service the hotel guest expects becomes more highly personalized.

Guests always react in many ways in similar cases of inconvenience, so there can never be a standard answer to a particular problem. Small problems tend to escalate as the day goes on, and small problems eventually become big problems. By handling small problems with patience, attention, and empathy, one can prevent bigger problems, ensuring satisfaction and preventing legal complaints. The key to forming this kind of problem-solving is that staff should exercise empathy toward the guests and listen carefully to them. Perhaps asking both parties if there is anything else that they can do for them also helps. Asking both parties also suggests that you keep the mediator in full and impartial control of the discussion. In a hotel, the friendliness of the staff and the way that problems are handled play an important role in the success or failure of the property. Every staff member should be skilled in assisting guests in finding an acceptable solution to solve the guest's problem. This can mean giving a discount, finding/cleaning another room, entering into negotiations, or finding another solution to the problem. The cause of the problem is not important, but how the problem is eventually solved is.

Mediation is part of the dispute management systems designed to deal with disputes and areas of conflict within organizations. In the service industry where customer service and satisfaction are a priority, mediation can change the response to a service failure into a tool that reduces customer dissatisfaction, increases customer recovery, profitability, and customer retention. Mediation is the use of a third-party neutral in a dispute to assist disputants in finding their resolution. While mediation is often associated with labour and employment disputes, there is an increasing trend in organizations in business to use mediation also to resolve disputes and remedy conflicts involving customers, triangular conflicts, institutions having disputes or ongoing conflicts with other related entities.

15. Mediation and Contractual Disputes in the Hospitality Industry.

Business practices have changed over time, but contract disputes on the basis of breach come in all sizes and from many peccadilloes. In the classic one-size-fits-all construct of consumer contracts, buyers establish the amount and type of liability for sellers who may have contributed to product defects, non-performance, or other misrepresentations in proximity to distrustful and distressful states of mind. In breach cases, the principles apply regardless of whether the acquirers are companies or individuals – the buyer has the ultimate duty to verify and assure the products are workable for the vendor, not the other way around. Values of trust, teamwork, and context vs. individual responsibility have been viewed in different ways at different times depending on the undercurrents at the time.

When the basics have been disregarded, misunderstandings among the parties can lead to battles. Taking an example, In the UAE, April 2018, an individual signed an agreement with a tour company for hotel bookings over two years, paying Dh9,000 for six days/nights of stay per year. However, when attempting to use the service, they found the company's office closed and unresponsive. This situation left the individual unable to utilize the promised facilities, prompting them to seek recovery of the money paid.

Assuming both the individual and the tour company are based in Dubai, the provisions of Federal Law No. 5 of 1985 on Civil Transactions Law of the United Arab Emirates (the 'Civil Transactions Law') and Federal

Law No. 24 of 2006 on Consumer Protection ('Consumer Protection Law') are applicable. According to the Consumer Protection Law, a Consumer Protection Department is established under the Ministry of Economy where consumers can file complaints. Furthermore, Article 4 (6) of the Consumer Protection Law states: "A department shall be set up in the Ministry under the name of the Consumer Protection Department and shall carry out the following competencies: Receive consumers' complaints and adopt the procedures in this regard or refer them to the competent authorities. The complaint may be submitted directly by the consumer or filed by the consumer protection association as a representative of the complainant." Therefore, based on this provision, the individual can file a complaint against the company with the Consumer Protection Department located in the Department of Economy and Tourism (DET) office.

Moreover, under the Civil Transactions Law, parties to an agreement are obligated to perform the contract in good faith. Article 246 (1) states: "The contract shall be implemented according to the provisions contained therein and in a manner consistent with the requirements of good faith." It appears the tour company may not be acting in good faith, as they have been unresponsive and unavailable, preventing the individual from utilizing the promised facilities. Therefore, the individual's claim is further supported by the tour company's potential breach of good faith.

Given the amount paid is Dh9,000, it is advisable for the individual to file a civil complaint against the company at the Centre for Amicable Settlement of Disputes at Dubai Court (the 'Centre'). The Centre handles debts/claims under Dh50,000. When filing the complaint, the individual should bring any supporting documents, such as the agreement and proof of payment, to the Centre for registering the civil complaint. They may approach the Centre for further details.

Opting for an amicable resolution through the Centre for Amicable Settlement of Disputes offers several benefits over litigation. Firstly, it is cost-effective, significantly reducing legal costs and making it an affordable option for recovering smaller amounts. Furthermore, it is time-efficient, as amicable settlements are generally faster, avoiding the lengthy process of traditional court proceedings. Additionally, this approach preserves relationships by fostering a cooperative rather than adversarial approach, which can help maintain business relationships. Lastly, it allows for more creative and flexible solutions that a court might not provide.

In conclusion, pursuing an amicable resolution can expedite the recovery of funds, minimize expenses, and maintain a positive approach to conflict resolution. Therefore, the individual stands to benefit significantly from choosing this method to resolve their dispute with the tour company.

Contractual disputes can arise not only between an individual and a hospitality company but also between employers and employees regarding their contractual obligations towards each other. For example, non-compete clauses in employment contracts can sometimes be unfair. An employee might be restricted from working in their industry for a significant period after leaving a job, which can severely limit their career opportunities and livelihood. Conversely, an overly broad non-compete clause might prevent an employer from protecting their business interests effectively. These clauses can lead to disputes if either party feels the terms are unreasonable or excessively restrictive, However, the enforceability and prospects of success of a legal remedy in the event of a breach of a post-contractual non-compete clause have always been legally difficult. Experience has shown that the legal enforcement is usually a lengthy and costly process, particularly in circumstances where a breach of the post-contractual non-compete clause is imminent, i.e. between the signing of a new employment contract and the actual start of employment, a preventive injunction often appears to be the most effective remedy. However, except for the legislatures of certain free zones, the UAE jurisdiction lacks such a right and remedy. Therefore, an imminent or even foreseeable violation cannot be prevented by law, leaving only the possibility of asserting a claim for damages. In this context, however, the burden of proof is on the employer with regard to the damage suffered, which is also difficult to quantify and specify in individual cases.[27]

The Ministry of HRs and Emiratisation (MoHRE) has implemented a new process effective from 1 January 2024, allowing for the resolution of disputes amounting to AED50,000 or less concerning private sector companies, workers, domestic workers, and recruitment agencies. This streamlined approach aims to save time and effort for all parties involved by providing final executive decisions on disputes, including those related to non-compliance with previous settlement decisions. The updated mechanism aligns with recent legislative amendments and empowers both parties to file a lawsuit before the Court of Appeals within 15 working days if unsatisfied with the Ministry's decision. Furthermore, the Ministry will continue its efforts to reach amicable settlements for disputes exceeding AED50,000, with unresolved cases being referred to the relevant court for resolution within a maximum of 15 working days. These amendments are designed to enhance compliance with legal obligations, reduce the number of irregular workers, and contribute to the UAE's global competitiveness by expediting the resolution of labour disputes within a fair and transparent legislative environment. This initiative builds on the UAE's top ranking for lack of labour disputes in the IMD World Competitiveness Yearbook 2022, reinforcing its commitment to integrity and impartiality in resolving employment-related conflicts.[28]

16. Mediation and Intellectual Property Issues in the Hospitality Industry.

The dispute resolution process typically involves mediation and/or arbitration, focusing on trademarks or safety intellectual property (patents). For instance, in the hospitality industry, a dispute over a trademark for a popular hotel chain and restaurants can significantly impact the company's reputation and its future business prospects. In most cases, when a contractual breach occurs in an industry dominated by hospitality, the affected brands and products have the potential to disrupt the company's reputation. For example, if a well-known restaurant chain faces a patent dispute over a unique cooking process, this could deter future collaborations or investments, leading to direct financial losses from the time consumed from filing the case to the court decision. In the popular case of NY Pizzeria, Inc. v Syal, the famous Italian restaurant chain claimed that the defendant had infringed their intellectual property rights by copying the same flavours and taste in their recipes and plating. However, the court observed that in this case, Plaintiff failed to identify the secondary function of the elements of this dish, such as ziti, eggplant, and chicken, and thus dismissed their claims. This case was filed in September 17, 2013 and the decision was on October 20, 2014 which took almost a year for having a court decision. Even if litigation or arbitration is the resolution method adopted by the parties, foreign neutral companies, mediators, judges, and arbitrators must remember that the time-sensitive environment affecting the success and longevity of the hospitality industry remains critical.

As in Case Standard International Management v EUIPO Case T-768/20 (July 2022), Standard International Management LLC engaged in a protracted legal battle, culminating in a judgment issued by the General Court on July 13, 2022. The case originated from the revocation proceedings initiated by Asia Standard Management Services Ltd on October 10, 2018, against Standard International's EU figurative mark, "The Standard." The dispute began when Hotelsab LLC, Standard International's predecessor, filed the mark's registration application on June 16, 2009. Despite the mark being registered on July 8, 2011, Asia Standard sought its revocation, initiating a lengthy legal process. Following the Cancellation Division's decision to revoke the mark on March 2, 2020, Standard International appealed on May 4, 2020. After a hearing on November 17, 2021, the General Court delivered its judgment, affirming the Board of Appeal's decision due to insufficient evidence of genuine use of the mark in the EU. This case underscores the complexities inherent in defending a trademark against revocation, especially in a prolonged litigation process.

---

27 Rödl & Partner UAE: Employee Non-Compete Clauses | Published on 22 November 2023
28 MoHRE To Resolve AED50,000 Or Less Disputes with Final Executive Decisions As Of 1 January 2024, Aiming To Expedite Collection Of Legal Entitlements

Patent registration in the UAE is a long and elaborate process. The process takes a long time in most other jurisdictions as well. Sometimes, the life cycle of a product may expire by the time a patent is granted. This is one of the reasons why patents remain overlooked in the food and beverage (F&B) industry. However, this should not become a reason for ruling out the relevance of patents in the food industry. A patent can still provide benefits even when an application is pending.

For example, competitors may think twice before launching a similar product when they learn about your patent application. There is uncertainty in the final scope of the patent until it has been granted, keeping competitors on their toes. If competitors plan to file a patent application, having your application in place puts you in a strong position in the case of a dispute. This uncertainty can act as a deterrent and provide a strategic advantage in maintaining market position.

In the realm of hospitality, the presence of in-house mediators is not yet widespread, despite the industry's growing recognition of the need for swift, informal, and cost-effective dispute resolution to uphold customer satisfaction and avoid prolonged legal battles. However, there is a growing realization of the importance of incorporating such practices within the hospitality sector. Many establishments are now considering the adoption of in-house mediation programs to address conflicts efficiently and maintain positive guest experiences. These mediators, although not yet universally adopted, hold potential for transforming the industry's approach to dispute resolution, offering a proactive means of resolving issues before they escalate. By embracing in-house mediation, hospitality businesses can foster a culture of collaboration, enhance customer service, and mitigate the risks associated with lengthy litigation processes. This approach aligns with the broader trend towards ADR methods, as suggested by Bessemer in a 2005 study. Bessemer's study proposed that historical conflicts, such as those between Sparta and Athens, might have found resolution through mediation by smaller Greek cities, underscoring the effectiveness of mediation in promoting reconciliation and preserving relationships. With this perspective in mind, one wonders: Could mediation similarly serve as a pivotal tool in the hospitality industry, facilitating the effective management of disputes and the sustenance of harmonious business relationships?

17. Mediation and Environmental Concerns in the Hospitality Industry.

In response to global sustainability initiatives, the hospitality industry must prioritize energy conservation, waste management, and water conservation/recycling. Hoteliers, who depend on delivering exceptional service to attract tourists, face increasing challenges in meeting these demands. For example,

Collaborating with a company to transform atmospheric humidity into pure drinking water, the Delta Dubai Investment Park, under the leadership of Sandeep Walia, Marriott International's COO in the Middle East, launched the AirOWater system project, aiming to generate 500 to 1,000 liters of water daily, a sustainable effort underscored by the group's commitment to eliminating single-use plastics. Other hotels like W Dubai – Mina Seyahi, Le Meridien Mina Seyahi Beach Resort & Waterpark, and The Westin Dubai Mina Seyahi Beach Resort & Marina have implemented similar initiatives, with on-site bottling plants providing fresh, filtered water. This endeavour, in partnership with BE WTR, seeks to remove 1.5 million plastic bottles annually. Additionally, The Abu Dhabi Edition produces 500 bottles of still and sparkling water daily, showcasing a commitment to sustainability. Meanwhile, the Marriott Resort Palm Jumeirah utilizes solar panels to heat water in guest rooms and the hotel spa, a measure complemented by a heat pump that creates chilled water for air conditioning. Addressing food waste, The Ritz-Carlton Dubai, JBR opened a vertical hydroponic farm last year, yielding fresh produce while conserving water. These programs, while commendable, pose significant challenges to hoteliers, particularly in terms of implementation costs, technological adoption, and maintaining operational efficiency amidst sustainability efforts.

A different study, encompassing 200 upscale European hotel guests from the UK, highlighted a favourable correlation between green marketing efforts and guest satisfaction with eco-friendly practices [29]. The findings revealed that portraying an environmentally conscious image positively influences guests' loyalty to the hotel, leading to heightened levels of trust and satisfaction. The promotion of eco-friendly initiatives has emerged as a pivotal strategy in attracting environmentally conscious consumers, enriching their overall stay, and bolstering their loyalty, thereby elevating the likelihood of their return visits, recommendations, and positive word-of-mouth advertising for the hotel.

For guests, the shift towards eco-conscious hospitality can significantly influence their experience and perception of a hotel. Imagine a guest checking into a hotel equipped with energy-efficient lighting, water-saving fixtures, and recycling programs. These initiatives not only align with their personal values but also enhance their overall satisfaction with the stay. On the other hand, if a guest notices discrepancies between the hotel's sustainability claims and its actual practices, it can lead to disappointment and distrust. For instance, if a hotel promotes itself as plastic-free but continues to use single-use plastics in guest amenities, it can undermine the guest's confidence in the hotel's commitment to sustainability.

Similarly, hotel managers face multifaceted challenges in implementing and maintaining sustainability programs. Consider the financial aspect: investing in renewable energy systems, water conservation technologies, and waste management infrastructure requires a substantial upfront capital outlay. While these investments may yield long-term cost savings through reduced utility bills and operational expenses, they can strain the hotel's budget in the short term. Moreover, ensuring compliance with sustainability standards and regulations adds another layer of complexity for hotel managers. They must navigate a maze of environmental guidelines while balancing operational efficiency and guest satisfaction.

In such scenarios, mediation can serve as a valuable tool for addressing conflicts and finding mutually acceptable solutions. For example, if guests express concerns about the hotel's sustainability practices, mediation provides a platform for open dialogue between guests and management. Through facilitated discussions, both parties can voice their perspectives, identify common goals, explore practical solutions and avoid future negative online reviews. This collaborative approach not only resolves immediate issues but also fosters a sense of trust and transparency between the hotel and its guests.

Furthermore, mediation can help hotel managers navigate internal conflicts related to sustainability initiatives. For instance, when a hotel decides to implement new eco-friendly practices, such as reducing plastic use, conserving water, or sourcing local organic food, it often requires significant changes in operations and employee behaviour. These changes can sometimes lead to disagreements among staff members. For example, the housekeeping team might resist the move to eliminate single-use plastic toiletries due to concerns about increased workload and the time needed to refill reusable dispensers. Similarly, the kitchen staff might have reservations about sourcing local organic food due to perceived higher costs or concerns about consistent supply.

In such scenarios, mediation can play a crucial role. A mediator can facilitate open discussions where all parties can express their concerns and perspectives. Through mediation, the hotel manager can ensure that everyone's voice is heard and that any misconceptions are clarified. For instance, the mediator can help the housekeeping team understand the long-term environmental benefits and potential cost savings of reducing plastic use. At the same time, the kitchen staff can be reassured about the feasibility and advantages of sourcing local food, such as fresher ingredients and supporting the local economy. By addressing these concerns through a structured mediation process, the hotel can find mutually agreeable solutions. This might include providing additional training for the housekeeping team to streamline the refilling process or negotiating with local suppliers to ensure a steady supply of organic produce at competitive prices.

---

29 Assaker, G.; O'Connor, P.; El-Haddad, R. Examining an integrated model of the green image, perceived quality, satisfaction, trust, and loyalty in upscale hotels. J. Hosp. Mark. Manag. 2020, 29, 934–955. [Google Scholar]

Moreover, mediation helps in building a culture of collaboration and mutual respect among staff members. It fosters a sense of shared purpose and commitment to the hotel's sustainability goals. When employees feel involved in the decision-making process and understand the broader impact of their actions, they are more likely to support and actively participate in sustainability initiatives.

Overall, mediation empowers stakeholders in the hospitality industry to navigate the complexities of sustainability while promoting positive guest experiences and operational efficiency. By embracing mediation as a conflict resolution strategy, hotels can strengthen their commitment to environmental responsibility and enhance their reputation as socially conscious establishments.

18. Mediation and Technology-Related Disputes in the Hospitality Industry.

In the global commercial and technology-driven environment, the travel and hospitality industry is increasingly susceptible to technology disputes. As the sector relies more on computerized systems and sophisticated check-in procedures, conflicts become more likely. For example, the popularity of selecting a room and checking in using a kiosk upon arrival is rising. However, this technology might fail in specific travel situations, such as when a traveller uses a coupon, has open questions that need answers, or has needs that cannot be met by technology alone. Problems related to the use of kiosks and other advanced guest interfaces, such as iPads to enhance guest experience in hotels, can lead to conflicts between hoteliers and their guests. Consequently, disputes over guest interactions often arise when technology is involved in travel tourism.

The hospitality industry can be a prime location for technology-related disputes, including disagreements over various aspects of the hotel registration process. Both the hotel and the guest have certain rights and obligations when a room is booked. Laws in many jurisdictions require hotels to enforce local laws and regulations, making it essential for both hoteliers and guests to understand specific local rules. In such cases, where disputes arise, mediation rather than litigation or arbitration can be particularly effective in resolving these issues, thus preserving and potentially even enhancing relationships. Indeed, mediation may be generally preferred by the hospitality industry to resolve issues that arise between hotels and their guests and between others who have business connections to a hotel.

From my perspective, mediation is especially valuable because the GM often cannot resolve these issues alone. The GM may be deeply embedded in the system and familiar with operational protocols but often lacks the neutrality and specialized training that a mediator brings. They may also become frustrated or overwhelmed by the rapid changes and complexities of new technology features, leading to blind spots in addressing conflicts effectively.

While an IT specialist has the technical expertise to address and resolve many issues, they might not have the skills to mediate between parties with conflicting interests or emotional investments in the outcome. The IT department can certainly troubleshoot and fix technical problems, but their focus is generally on resolving the technical aspects rather than the relational or contractual nuances of a dispute. Moreover, IT specialists might lack the authority to make decisions that satisfy all parties involved, such as offering compensation or changing operational policies.

A mediator, on the other hand, brings a unique set of skills and attributes that make them particularly effective in resolving such disputes. Mediators are trained to remain neutral, ensuring that all parties feel heard and understood. This neutrality helps in defusing tensions and fostering a cooperative atmosphere. Additionally, mediators possess strong emotional intelligence, enabling them to navigate the emotional aspects of conflicts, which the GM or IT specialists might find challenging. They can identify underlying issues and address emotional needs, which are often pivotal in reaching a satisfactory resolution.

Furthermore, mediators are skilled in conflict resolution techniques that go beyond technical problem-solving. They facilitate open communication, help clarify misunderstandings, and guide parties toward mutually acceptable solutions. Their ability to see the broader picture and understand the interests of all parties involved allows them to craft creative solutions that might not be immediately apparent to those entrenched in the conflict.

For instance, consider a scenario where a hotel implements a new self-service check-in kiosk system. Guests are encouraged to use this technology to select their rooms, check in, and receive their room keys. However, a guest with a specific room request due to a medical condition finds that the kiosk cannot accommodate their needs, leading to frustration and a potential conflict with hotel staff. While the GM might be aware of the technology, they might not fully understand its limitations or be able to see an unbiased solution due to their vested interest in the system's success.

In this situation, a mediator organizes a meeting with the guest, the hotel management, and an IT representative to understand the issue from all perspectives. By facilitating an open dialogue, the mediator allows the guest to explain their medical condition and specific room requirements while the hotel management and IT explain the current limitations of the kiosk system. This collaborative problem-solving helps both parties brainstorm possible solutions, such as assigning a staff member to assist guests with special needs during check-in or modifying the kiosk system to include a special requests option. Ultimately, the hotel agrees to immediately assign a staff member for assistance and commits to updating the kiosk software within a specific timeframe. As a result, the guest feels heard and accommodated, the hotel's reputation is preserved, and the technology system is improved for future guests.

Another example involves in-room technology issues. Suppose a hotel introduces tablets in rooms for ordering room service and controlling room settings. A guest finds the tablet interface confusing and unresponsive, resulting in a poor experience. The GM, familiar with the intended benefits of the tablets, may become frustrated when guests do not embrace the new technology. Here, mediation can play a crucial role. The mediator gathers detailed information about the guest's experience and the hotel's perspective on the technology's intended use. By encouraging both parties to discuss the specific issues with the tablet interface, the mediator facilitates the exploration of solutions such as providing a user manual in the room, offering an alternative method to request services (e.g., a dedicated phone line), and scheduling regular updates and testing of the tablet software. Consequently, the guest's immediate needs are met, and the hotel improves its technology based on real user feedback, enhancing overall guest satisfaction.

Mediation can also be beneficial in resolving booking system failures. For example, if a hotel's new online booking system double-books rooms, leading to a guest being turned away upon arrival, mediation can help. The GM might struggle with these situations due to a lack of technical expertise or the emotional stress of handling dissatisfied guests. The IT department might fix the double-booking issue technically but addressing the guest's dissatisfaction and preventing future conflicts requires more than a technical solution. The mediator meets with the affected guest and hotel management to discuss the incident and its impact. By helping to identify the root cause of the double-booking issue with input from the hotel's IT team, the mediator facilitates discussions to develop an immediate resolution, such as arranging alternative accommodations for the guest at no extra cost and providing additional perks like free meals or spa services. The hotel also commits to conducting a comprehensive review of the booking system and implementing safeguards to prevent future occurrences. Thus, the guest's immediate inconvenience is addressed, and the hotel takes steps to ensure such issues do not recur, maintaining trust and loyalty.

Finally, consider a scenario where a hotel contracts a tech company to install an advanced security system, but the implementation faces delays and technical issues, causing operational disruptions. The GM, focused on maintaining day-to-day operations, may not have the bandwidth to address the technical intricacies of the delay. The IT team might be heavily involved in resolving technical aspects but lacks the authority to negotiate contract terms or make decisions about compensations. Mediation can bring representatives from the hotel, the tech company, and the IT department together to discuss the issues. By clarifying the original expectations and the current state of the project, the mediator highlights areas of miscommunication. Through negotiation, both parties agree on a revised timeline, additional support from the tech company, and potential compensation for the delays. They establish a protocol for ongoing communication to monitor progress and address any future issues promptly. This leads to a mutually satisfactory agreement, ensuring the project's successful completion and preserving the business relationship.

By opting for mediation, the hospitality industry can address conflicts efficiently, saving time and resources that would otherwise be spent on prolonged legal battles. Mediation fosters open communication and collaboration, leading to creative solutions that satisfy all parties involved. This approach not only resolves disputes but also strengthens relationships, enhances trust, and promotes a positive image for the hotel.

In conclusion, while the GM and IT specialists play crucial roles within a hotel, they often face limitations in resolving conflicts that involve both technical and relational aspects. Mediation provides an effective solution by combining technical understanding with impartial conflict resolution skills, ensuring that disputes are resolved in a way that maintains guest satisfaction and operational harmony.

19. Mediation and Workplace Diversity in the Hospitality Industry.

Mediation proves beneficial in resolving conflicts between hotel departments, such as the housekeeping and front desk teams having a misunderstanding about room readiness schedules, leading to delays and guest dissatisfaction. Through mediation, representatives from both departments can discuss their operational challenges and develop a coordinated plan, ensuring rooms are cleaned and inspected promptly before check-in times, thereby streamlining operations and enhancing the overall guest experience with timely and efficient service. Additionally, mediation addresses conflicts between the food and beverage department and the event planning team, where scheduling conflicts may overwhelm kitchen staff and impact service quality. Similarly, unexpected maintenance issues can be resolved by establishing a communication protocol between the maintenance team and the front desk, ensuring guests are promptly informed and alternative arrangements made. In the hospitality industry, particularly in the Gulf region like Saudi Arabia (KSA), Kuwait (KW), Oman, and UAE, tasks are typically handled by employees from different cultures, languages, and accents, leading to conflicts and communication barriers. These barriers often result in delayed or incomplete information exchange, with some parties relying on others' intellectuality to address issues adequately. Cultural, behavioural, and religious attributes further complicate communication, sometimes leading to intentional avoidance of communication or reliance on intermediaries. Such diversity-related communication challenges prolong conflict resolution and may even impact guest experience, leading to negative reviews that tarnish the hotel or restaurant's reputation over time.

Most probably, in these kinds of conflicts, the management takes three decisions called the 3Ts (Train, Transfer, and Terminate). Usually, these actions are the most preventive measures that the management takes to avoid these kinds of disputes. In small chains where they lack a training manager and proper HR, and where the hotel is run by the GM (a one-man show culture), they probably have only one "T," which is Terminate. Probably, the diversity of culture must be acquainted with strong policies and procedures that need to be followed by all staff working in the hotel. The role of HR is to facilitate these policies to all staff members at different levels. However, some HRs and training managers may design policies and procedures facilitated by training courses that demonstrate them in a workshop environment, especially for blue-collar staff. They may not invite white-collar employees to such courses because they perceive their level to be higher, even though sometimes the training managers and HR may facilitate such training with the presence of the GM or other white-collar employees who may lack knowledge of such training, distracting the blue-collar staff's attention and leaving them with no knowledge of the company's policies and procedures. Over time, this can lead to more conflicts between peers and even between managers and their subordinates. I have seen some staff who are more knowledgeable about the company's policies and procedures than their managers, and sometimes when disputes arise between them, both parties refer to the policies and procedures, with the staff member often prevailing.

These consequences are more to be avoided by properly understanding the multicultural environment that the hotel encompasses. Indians, Egyptians, Lebanese, Pakistanis, French, English, and you name it, all these cultures may not adhere to certain policies and procedures unless they are strongly assigned from the management company to all its employees, regardless of their positions or tenure within the company. Any new policy from the management company must undergo specific implementation phases across all the hotels or restaurants under the operator's management. Marriott, Accor, and IHG, for example, have strong policies and procedures that are followed not only among staff and their managers but also across regions.

The role of the mediator here lies not only in mediating between parties to reach a settlement but also in guiding the management company to better address cultural norms within its policies and procedures. This involves adding their own guidelines to ensure not only compliance with the policies and procedures but also understanding their right to mediation if any conflict arises. This type of implementation needs to be carefully structured to prevent employees and staff members, whether white or blue-collar, from using their rights to mediation directly without first aligning with the policies and procedures. Ensuring alignment before escalating to conflict resolution by mediators is crucial. Such Key Performance Indicators (KPIs) need to be well implemented by a committee composed of executive employees from the management company, including those from operations, HR, and learning and development. This committee will not only ensure the execution of the guidelines but also provide KPIs for performance evaluation.

For example, to ensure the successful implementation of mediation guidelines and the improvement of inter-departmental coordination, a variety of KPIs should be established. These KPIs can be linked to the Balanced Scorecard framework, which focuses on four perspectives: Financial, Customer, Internal Processes, and Learning & Growth. For instance, in resolving conflicts between the housekeeping and front desk teams over room readiness schedules, in order for the mediator to first asses their performance related to the balanced score card before leading to conflict resolution process directly, they must evaluate the Financial Perspective that include measuring cost savings, tracking the impact of improved room readiness on overall revenue with a focus on guest retention and repeat bookings. The Customer Perspective could involve monitoring guest satisfaction ratings related to room readiness and check-in experience, measuring the average time to resolve guest complaints, and assessing the likelihood of guests recommending the hotel based on their experience with timely room availability. The Internal Processes Perspective could track the average time it takes for rooms to be cleaned, inspected, and ready for check-in, measure the percentage of guests able to check in on time, and evaluate the frequency and effectiveness of meetings between housekeeping and front desk teams, tracking the number of resolved conflicts. The Learning & Growth Perspective could include, measuring employee satisfaction and engagement levels, and assessing improvements in employees' conflict resolution skills through regular evaluations and feedback sessions. By implementing these KPIs and linking them to the Balanced Scorecard, the hotel can ensure a structured approach and even save of the time of the mediator when it comes to resolving conflicts. These overall policies and procedures buoyed by the mediation guidelines will foster the collaboration between all the departments to ensure their efficiency within the organization.

20. Mediation and International Disputes in the Hospitality Industry.

Relevant hotel and restaurant laws serve as a framework worldwide, operating within each country's jurisdiction to regulate how disputes within the hospitality industry are addressed. These laws are crucial for resolving issues when guests encounter problems at hotels or restaurants. In the United States, laws such as the Americans with Disabilities Act (ADA) ensure accessibility for all guests, while consumer protection laws safeguard against fraudulent practices. Similarly, in the European Union, regulations like the General Data Protection Regulation (GDPR) protect guests' privacy rights. In the United Kingdom, the Consumer Protection Act 2015 establishes consumer rights, ensuring goods and services meet acceptable standards and are provided at the declared price. Meanwhile, in the United Arab Emirates, the Consumer Protection Law, established through Federal Decree Law No. 5 of 2023 amending the Federal Law No. 15 of 2020, aims to protect consumer rights, including the right to quality goods and services at declared prices. It also prioritizes consumer health and safety and prohibits suppliers from misusing consumer data for marketing purposes. These legal frameworks provide a foundation for addressing disputes effectively and fairly. However, hoteliers and guests also have the flexibility to tailor dispute resolution methods to their specific needs and preferences by including clauses in their contracts. By incorporating dispute resolution clauses, parties can opt for mediation, arbitration, or traditional court litigation as the chosen method for resolving particular disputes. This flexibility allows for customized approaches to dispute resolution, catering to the unique circumstances of each situation and promoting efficient and satisfactory outcomes for all involved parties.

A. *Resolving Hotel Management Agreement Disputes.*

In the international hospitality industry, Hotel Management Agreements (HMAs) play a pivotal role in defining the relationship between hotel owners and operators. However, these agreements often entail fixed terms for base management fees, incentive fees, and other marketing fees, leaving little room for negotiation based on market trends, cultural nuances, and competitive landscapes. Some HMAs extend over long periods, spanning up to 20 years, and owners may find themselves bound by terms that become increasingly unfavourable, especially during challenging market conditions such as the COVID-19 pandemic. This can lead to frustration for owners, who may see their expected profits diminished compared to initial projections set by the operator.

On the other hand, operators face challenges as well, with market downturns compelling them to either withdraw from the market or renegotiate agreements with owners to align with contract terms. Disputes arising from these agreements, if pursued through litigation, can prolong resolution timelines, and incur substantial costs. Moreover, not all lawyers or courts possess expertise in the commercial intricacies of HMAs, necessitating the involvement of specialists. Meanwhile, prolonged litigation can adversely affect hotel operations, eroding profits and tarnishing reputations for both owners and operators.

in the context of Hotel Management Agreements (HMAs), incorporating clauses related to the General Data Protection Regulation (GDPR) is essential, particularly regarding data privacy and confidentiality. These clauses outline responsibilities for both the hotel operator and the owner in adhering to GDPR regulations, specifying data protection measures, encryption protocols, access controls, and procedures for handling data breaches. Additionally, confidentiality and non-disclosure clauses are included to prevent unauthorized access or disclosure of sensitive information, such as guests' personal data and proprietary business information. Owners in the Gulf Cooperation Council (GCC) market, often characterized by high-net-worth individuals or prominent entities, may have distinct concerns regarding GDPR compliance compared to individual or family-owned hotels in Europe. Despite the GDPR's aim to standardize data protection laws, its application in the GCC region may vary based on local regulations, cultural norms, and business practices. Negotiation and customization of GDPR clauses in HMAs become crucial for aligning with local laws and business practices, addressing unique needs and sensitivities while ensuring adequate protection of guests' personal data.

Mediation emerges as a viable solution to mitigate disputes stemming from HMAs. By engaging experts well-versed in hospitality dynamics, mediation offers a platform for timely and adequate resolution of issues. Mediators with industry-specific knowledge can effectively navigate complexities inherent in HMAs, facilitating constructive dialogue between parties. Through mediation, disputes related to base management fees, incentive fees, and marketing fees can be addressed efficiently, allowing owners and operators to find mutually beneficial solutions while preserving their long-term relationship and the profitability of the hotel. Moreover, mediation offers a more expedient and cost-effective alternative to litigation, sparing both parties from protracted legal battles and enabling them to focus on operational excellence and guest satisfaction.

B. *Disputes Over Contractual Obligations.*

Disputes over contractual obligations in the hospitality industry can often involve complex issues related to supply chains and distribution channels, significantly impacting business operations. For instance, consider a restaurant located in London, UK, facing severe disruptions due to its supplier's failure to meet delivery obligations. This situation not only breaches the Consumer Protection Act 2015 but also threatens the restaurant's ability to serve its customers. The complication intensifies as the restaurant is part of a hotel managed by a management company, requiring the resolution of contractual disputes between the restaurant owner and the management company.

In this case, the supplier was contractually responsible for all actions of third-party distribution channels. However, delays were extensive, primarily due to inefficiencies in these channels. The supplier attempted to invoke the force majeure clause, arguing that uncontrollable events were causing the delays. However, the lapse of time between the supplier and the third-party distribution channel was evident, and upon investigation, it was found that force majeure did not apply as the delays were due to negligence rather than unforeseen circumstances.

Initially, this dispute seemed destined for the courts in the UK, potentially invoking the Consumer Protection Act 2015. However, before it escalated to litigation, which could be time-consuming and costly, the parties agreed to mediation. They hired an expert mediator who specialized in contractual disputes. The mediator facilitated discussions between the restaurant, the supplier, and the management company, focusing on identifying the root cause of the delays and finding a workable solution.

During mediation, it was revealed that the supplier's oversight of the third-party distribution channels was lacking, contributing significantly to the delays. The mediator proposed a settlement that added value to all parties involved. The supplier agreed to provide additional services, including covering other branches of the restaurant chain across the UK for the rest of the year. Furthermore, the supplier committed to a guarantee ensuring no future negligence in handling the distribution channels, effectively preventing similar issues.

This mediation not only resolved the immediate dispute but also established a framework for better future collaboration. The supplier's commitment to improved service and accountability reassured the restaurant and the management company, while the added value service of covering other branches enhanced the restaurant chain's operational efficiency and customer satisfaction. The solution avoided the lengthy court process and aligned with the principles of the Consumer Protection Act 2015, ensuring that consumer rights were upheld without the need for litigation.

21. Mediation and Brand Reputation in the Hospitality Industry.

In industries such as hospitality, and entertainment, where businesses rely heavily on customer satisfaction and brand reputation, the need for rapid dispute resolution is paramount. From my perspective and experience, I've witnessed firsthand how delays in resolving disputes can have cascading effects on daily operations. For instance, in the hospitality sector, a dispute over branding or franchise rights can disrupt marketing campaigns and impact guest loyalty. In such fast-paced industries, where opportunities can arise and disappear in the blink of an eye, there's little tolerance for prolonged legal battles.

In this scenario, imagine a hotel franchisee operating under the umbrella of a well-known brand. The franchisee, eager to stay competitive in the market, seeks to implement innovative marketing strategies to attract guests and boost revenue instead of the restricting marketing campaigns that the franchisee receive from the operator. However, tensions arise when the franchisor, who holds the branding rights and provides marketing support, disagrees with the proposed strategies and asks for more flexibility. The franchisee perception about marketing that in today's dynamic market, where consumer preferences shift rapidly, the timely execution of marketing campaigns is crucial to staying ahead of the competition and must be flexible with the market. Yet, the franchisee is obliged by a franchise agreement where they have to comply with the marketing standards of the franchisor. Therefore, the franchisee's hands are tied, and their ability to effectively promote the hotel's offerings is compromised. As a result, the franchisee faces the risk of losing potential guests to competitors and suffering a decline in revenue. Recognizing the urgency of the situation, the franchisee realizes the importance of resolving the dispute swiftly to mitigate financial losses and uphold the hotel's reputation as a reputable destination for travellers and seek flexibility in some marketing campaigns. Both parties agreed to hire a mediator as a neutral party that can guide them for more creative idea that can strengthen their grounds and help them keep the business relationship ongoing and each party can benefit from the solutions.

During the mediation sessions, orchestrated by the mediator, one solution that emerged was the concept of establishing a "Marketing Experimentation Zone" within the franchise agreement. The franchisee championed this idea, viewing it as a playground for testing novel marketing strategies, which could potentially attract new customers and boost revenue streams. However, the franchisor approached this idea with caution, expressing concerns about maintaining brand consistency and control. They feared that allowing too much flexibility could dilute the established brand identity or lead to inconsistent messaging, posing risks to the brand's reputation.

Conversely, the franchisor advocated for a more rigid marketing approach, emphasizing the importance of upholding brand standards and ensuring consistency across all franchise locations. While this approach offered the reassurance of brand integrity and customer loyalty, it also posed challenges in terms of adaptability and innovation. The franchisee worried that rigid marketing guidelines might hinder their ability to respond promptly to evolving market trends and consumer preferences.

Navigating through these divergent perspectives required adept mediation skills. The mediator validated each party's viewpoints, acknowledging the validity of their concerns and aspirations and to bridge the gap between the franchisee and franchisor, the mediator employed various conflict resolution techniques. The mediator guided the parties towards a agreement. Eventually, both the franchisee and franchisor may embrace the concept of a "Marketing Experimentation Zone," recognizing its potential to foster creativity while safeguarding brand reputation in a certain timeframe, where both parties can work collaboratively towards the success of the new settlement and then check the outcome and evaluate it. The mediator also mentioned if the concept worked well then they can introduce them within all their franchise contracts, allowing other franchisee to benefit from such settlement creating more flexible world according to the new trends.

Flexibility emerges as a cornerstone, with the franchisor demonstrating a willingness to adapt strategies to accommodate shifting industry dynamics. Compromise becomes key, as concessions are made on both sides to reach a middle ground conducive to sustainable resolution. Throughout this process, contractual terms are revisited and refined as needed to ensure more flexibility. Beyond immediate resolution, the focus extends to fostering a long-term partnership built on trust, transparency, and shared goals. By nurturing this collaborative ethos, not only is the current dispute resolved effectively, but the foundation is laid for continued success and growth within the franchise system, strengthening brand reputation and viability in the marketplace.

22. Mediation and Financial Disputes in the Hospitality Industry.

The rapid growth of the mediation industry is largely due to its ability to quickly and efficiently resolve disputes. While some attribute this growth to legal aid schemes, which handle many individual consumer problems and promote alternative justice, I believe the real reason is our fast-paced, app-based world that demands instant responses. The global pandemic also played a role by putting many disputes on hold in courts and tribunals, making mediation an attractive option. Mediation offers a confidential, unbiased way to resolve various disputes that could become very complex.

For example, consider a hotel facing a financial dispute with a supplier over delayed payments. While it might seem that financial disputes are straightforward since "money is money," it's not that simple. Financial disputes often involve reputation, emotional stress, and uncertainty. In my experience, quick resolution is crucial in the hospitality industry to prevent damage to the hotel's reputation and ensure continued operations.

During a particularly challenging time, such as a peak holiday season, I witnessed a hotel in North Africa embroiled in a contractual dispute with a major tour operator. The issue revolved around over bookings and last-minute cancellations, significantly impacting the hotel's operations and guest satisfaction. The hotel had prepared for a surge in visitors, anticipating a revenue of $500,000 for the season. However, due to the over-bookings and cancellations, they were facing potential losses of up to $200,000.

The hotel's management, facing a significant financial hit and potential damage to their reputation, decided to pursue litigation against the tour operator. The legal proceedings were initiated with the hope of recouping the lost revenue and holding the tour operator accountable for the breach of contract. However, as the case progressed, several legal implications became apparent.

Firstly, the litigation process was lengthy and expensive. Legal fees quickly accumulated, with the hotel spending over $100,000 on attorneys and court costs. The prolonged nature of the court case meant that the hotel's management had to divert their attention from daily operations, further straining their resources. Additionally, the public nature of the court proceedings brought unwanted negative publicity, causing further reputational damage. Guests and potential customers became wary of booking with the hotel, fearing further disruptions.

Secondly, the tour operator countered the lawsuit by arguing that the over-bookings and cancellations were due to unforeseen circumstances beyond their control. They cited force majeure clauses in the contract, attempting to shift some of the liability away from themselves. This legal defense added complexity to the case, requiring extensive evidence and expert testimony to rebut. The hotel had to prove that the cancellations were due to negligence or mismanagement by the tour operator, which was not straightforward and added to the duration and cost of the litigation.

As the case dragged on, the financial strain on both parties increased. The hotel's potential recovery of $200,000 in lost revenue seemed less significant compared to the mounting legal expenses and ongoing operational disruptions. The tour operator also faced significant legal costs and the risk of a tarnished reputation, which could affect their relationships with other hotel partners.

Considering the dreadful situation, if both parties had initially opted for of ADR methods, the process could have offered a faster, confidential, and less expensive resolution. A mediator could have facilitated discussions, helping both parties understand each other's perspectives and financial constraints.

Through mediation, a potential settlement could have been reached where the tour operator agreed to compensate the hotel a portion of the lost revenue, say $150,000, and commit to a minimum booking guarantee for the next peak season. Additionally, the tour operator could have offered marketing support to the hotel, valued at an additional $50,000, to help recover lost business. The hotel, in return, could have agreed to provide a discount on future bookings made through the tour operator, ensuring continued collaboration and business.

In summary, the decision to pursue litigation resulted in high costs, prolonged uncertainty, and reputational damage for both parties. In contrast, mediation could have provided a more efficient and mutually beneficial resolution, preserving both financial interests and business relationships. This critical analysis highlights the importance of considering ADR methods, especially in the hospitality industry where timely and effective solutions are crucial.

23. Mediation and Regulatory Compliance in the Hospitality Industry.

The structure of hotels, each representing a complex entity, must meet diverse needs, especially those concerning safety regulations set by local and national authorities. While safety measures may not directly confer a competitive edge, they are essential for fostering tourist development by assuaging travellers' fears. Failure to adhere to safety standards can deter tourists or make them more cautious upon arrival, impacting the image and prosperity of countries and their tourist destinations. The varying hotel regulations set by local authorities entail different levels of responsibility and yield diverse impacts, prompting some national governments to streamline regulations to enhance effectiveness and reduce implementation costs.

Hospitality, closely linked and shaped by economic, cultural, and social dynamics, responding to tourists' demands and preferences for their holiday or business accommodations. For example, during peak tourist seasons, hotels experience a surge in bookings and must ensure compliance with safety regulations to accommodate the arrival of guests. For example The KSA government is urging Muslims embarking on the Hajj pilgrimage to follow strict guidelines for a safe and respectful journey. Key requirements include obtaining a Hajj permit to avoid fines and deportation, adhering to the proper ihram dress code, and following crowd-safety regulations. The government has also launched awareness campaigns and taken action against fake tour operators. This strict approach ensures the well-being and safety of all pilgrims, akin to how the hospitality industry must adhere to safety regulations during peak tourist seasons to accommodate guests. The balance of territories and the competitiveness of tourist offerings significantly influence countries' image and economic vitality. Hotels play a pivotal role in the tourism sector, contributing significantly to the overall tourist experience through the variety and quality of accommodations they offer.

Considering these complexities, ADR methods such as mediation emerge as potential avenues for resolving legal conflicts, including personal injury claims. However, the effectiveness of mediation in the hospitality sector warrants critical examination. For example, consider a scenario where a restaurant customer suffers food poisoning due to improper food handling. The restaurant management might opt for mediation to address the customer's claim swiftly and avoid the higher costs and potential reputational damage of a court case. Mediation can provide a platform for the customer and the restaurant to reach a mutually agreeable settlement, often resulting in quicker compensation for the customer and less expense for the restaurant.

Nevertheless, this focus on cost-effective resolution can raise questions about fairness and justice. The injured customer might feel pressured to accept a settlement that is less than what they might receive through litigation, particularly if they lack legal representation during the mediation process. This could lead to a situation where the customer's long-term medical costs and other damages are not fully covered. Additionally, the restaurant might benefit from the private nature of mediation, avoiding public accountability for its negligence, which could have broader implications for public health and safety.

Such examples underscore the need to balance the benefits of mediation with the necessity of ensuring that it does not compromise the rights and well-being of injured parties. While mediation can offer a cost-effective and quicker resolution, it is crucial to implement safeguards that protect the interests of all parties involved and uphold principles of social justice. From my perspective, mediation, as an ADR method, holds promise for aligning societal justice goals with commercial imperatives within the hospitality sector. By facilitating efficient and mutually beneficial resolutions, mediation can address legal conflicts while preserving the interests of all stakeholders involved.

Furthermore, consider a hotel involved in a dispute with a guest who suffered an injury due to a slip-and-fall incident on the premises. Traditional litigation could result in prolonged legal proceedings, escalating costs, and reputational damage for both the hotel and the injured guest. However, through mediation, parties can engage in constructive dialogue facilitated by a neutral mediator to explore potential solutions. This collaborative approach allows the hotel to address the guest's concerns, offer appropriate compensation or remedies, and preserve its reputation while ensuring financial compensation for the injured party. In addition to financial compensation and improved safety measures, the hotel could offer the injured guest a comprehensive settlement package. This could include arranging for the guest's stay at a different hotel in another jurisdiction, along with covering the cost of airline tickets for the guest and their companions. Furthermore, the hotel could provide an upgrade or special amenities during the guest's stay at the alternative location to enhance their experience. Additionally, the hotel could offer to cover any medical expenses incurred by the guest during their treatment, including hospital stays until they are fit to travel back to their home country.

In return, the injured guest could provide positive feedback and high ratings for the hotel on platforms like Google Reviews or TripAdvisor, highlighting the hotel's commitment to guest safety and satisfaction. They could also provide assurances that they understand accidents can happen and appreciate the hotel's proactive steps to address the situation. Moreover, they could pledge to share their positive experience with others, thereby promoting the hotel's reputation and attracting future guests. Finally, the hotel could pledge in implementing and adhering to enhanced safety policies to prevent similar incidents in the future, demonstrating their willingness to ensure guest satisfaction and to provide a memorable stay of course in a positive way.

Through mediation, the hotel can demonstrate its commitment to addressing safety concerns, implementing corrective measures, and fostering a culture of accountability. By engaging in transparent and proactive dispute resolution, the hotel not only upholds societal justice goals but also mitigates potential financial losses and reputational harm.

In summary, mediation serves as a bridge between societal justice goals and commercial imperatives within the hospitality sector, offering a pragmatic approach to resolving legal conflicts while preserving business interests and promoting fairness. By embracing mediation as a proactive and collaborative dispute resolution mechanism, hotels can navigate legal challenges effectively, uphold ethical standards, and contribute to a more equitable and sustainable industry ecosystem.

24. Mediation and Corporate Social Responsibility in the Hospitality Industry.

In every industry, conflicts arise between businesses and their surroundings, requiring socially responsible responses. The hospitality sector, known for intangible experiences, often faces internal and community conflicts, impacting its reputation. Imagine a boutique hotel located in a picturesque coastal town. This hotel, known for its charm and ambiance, is a popular destination for travellers seeking a tranquil getaway. However, the idyllic atmosphere is disrupted when a nearby community raises concerns about the hotel's expansion plans, citing potential environmental harm and increased noise pollution.

Litigation Scenario:

In response to the community's objections, the hotel decides to pursue litigation to defend its expansion project. Legal proceedings ensue, leading to a prolonged and adversarial battle between the hotel and the community members. As the case drags on in court, media coverage intensifies, portraying the hotel as insensitive to environmental concerns and indifferent to community welfare.

The prolonged litigation not only tarnishes the hotel's reputation but also strains its relationship with the local community. Negative publicity affects bookings, leading to a decline in revenue. Moreover, the escalating legal fees and resources diverted to litigation drain the hotel's finances, impacting its ability to invest in sustainable practices and community initiatives.

ADR Scenario:

Alternatively, the hotel chooses to pursue mediation as a means of resolving the conflict amicably. In a mediation session facilitated by a neutral mediator, representatives from the hotel and the community come together to discuss their concerns and explore mutually acceptable solutions.

During mediation, the hotel acknowledges the community's environmental concerns and commits to implementing measures to mitigate noise pollution and minimize the ecological impact of its expansion. The hotel may take several proactive steps to mitigate its impact. Firstly, the hotel may invest in soundproofing technologies for its facilities, including guest rooms, event spaces, and entertainment areas, to minimize noise transmission to the surrounding community. Additionally, the hotel may establish strict noise control protocols and operational guidelines for its staff to adhere to, such as restricting outdoor activities during certain hours and enforcing quiet hours during the night.

Furthermore, the hotel would commit to conducting regular noise assessments and monitoring programs to ensure compliance with established noise levels and promptly address any noise disturbances that may arise. This proactive approach would demonstrate the hotel's commitment to minimizing its environmental footprint and addressing the concerns of the local community.

As part of the mediation agreement, the community may provide input on additional measures to mitigate noise pollution and enhance the overall quality of life for residents. For example, community members may propose the installation of noise barriers or landscaping features to further reduce noise levels, or advocate for the establishment of community liaison committees to facilitate ongoing communication and collaboration between the hotel and the surrounding neighbourhood. By incorporating community input into the mediation process, the hotel demonstrates its willingness to listen to and address the concerns of local residents, fostering greater trust and cooperation between the two parties.

As a result of the mediated settlement, the hotel and the community could reach a consensus that addresses both parties' interests. The hotel proceeds with its expansion project while incorporating environmentally sustainable practices, demonstrating its commitment to CSR. Positive media coverage highlights the collaborative efforts between the hotel and the community, enhancing the hotel's reputation and attracting eco-conscious travelers.

In summary, while litigation may escalate conflicts and strain relationships, mediation offers a constructive approach to resolving disputes in the hospitality sector. By embracing mediation and prioritizing CSR principles, hotels can mitigate conflicts, foster community engagement, and uphold their reputation as responsible corporate citizens.

25. Comparison of Litigation and Mediation in the Hospitality Industry.

1. *Introduction to Litigation and Mediation in the Hospitality Industry.*

Mediation is gaining popularity as a method for resolving disputes for several reasons. These include the rising cost of legal fees, the delays and loss of control associated with traditional legal processes, and the preference of some parties to work collaboratively toward a solution. The question arises as to whether mediation alone is more advantageous than purely litigious methods or a combination of litigation and mediation for resolving disputes in the hospitality industry.

There are several key factors driving the preference for mediation. Firstly, the cost of legal fees has been steadily increasing, making traditional litigation a more expensive option. Secondly, the legal process often involves significant delays, which can be frustrating and financially damaging for all parties involved. Mediation, on the other hand, tends to be faster and allows for more direct control over the outcome by the disputing parties. Additionally, mediation encourages a collaborative approach, which can preserve and even strengthen business relationships.

In the context of the hospitality industry, disputes often require swift and discreet resolutions to maintain customer satisfaction and protect business reputations. Mediation offers a confidential setting where parties can openly discuss issues and negotiate mutually beneficial solutions without the adversarial nature of a courtroom. This collaborative approach can lead to more creative and flexible resolutions that are tailored to the specific needs of the hospitality sector.

It is often said that a recession can be an advantage for law firms, as they are kept busy by clients seeking to enforce contracts and otherwise protect their positions. Litigation is often seen as one of the key functions of law firms. It is easy to understand why this is so: as an adjective, "litigious" implies a propensity to initiate legal proceedings, whether merited or not. As a noun, a "litigant" is a party to a lawsuit. Law firms litigate. Mediation, on the other hand, is often seen as an unfamiliar or even exotic concept. However, this situation is changing rapidly.

2. *Litigation and Mediation in the Hospitality Industry.*

There were several litigation cases in the hospitality industry, such as cases involving discrimination in employment such as In Thomson v. Little America Hotel, Co., the court granted summary judgment for the hotel, dismissing a discrimination claim from an employee terminated for performance issues without evidence of national origin bias. Moreover, in the context of business interruption due to covid such as in St. George Hotel Associates, LLC v. Affiliated FM Insurance Co., the court dismissed the hotel's claim for business interruption insurance, ruling that COVID-19 did not cause the required physical loss or damage to the property, and other cases related to negligence linked to the example described in the previous point *Mediation and Regulatory Compliance in the Hospitality Industry*, in Young v. BL Development, 2022 WL 422188, (2/11/22), bathmat issue. Plaintiff, a guest at defendant hotel, fell when a bathmat slipped beneath her feet in the tub. She sued for premises liability, hypothesizing that the hotel staff failed to ensure the mat was properly and securely suctioned when placed in the tub. The court granted summary judgment to the hotel noting that plaintiff did not offer any proof of what caused her fall. To claim that hotel staff improperly secured the mat in her tub is a just speculation.

Companies in the hospitality industry that may intend to use mediation services for dispute resolution were often seeking several benefits, including strengthening employer-employee relationships, saving on legal fees, obtaining immediate resolutions to issues, reaching business solutions, exploring non-conventional solutions, improving communication, maintaining confidentiality, and preserving the company's integrity. However, in my perspective, the legal systems of some companies in the past were not equipped to embrace mediation. Additionally, customers were often unaware of their rights against the management of hospitality organizations due to a lack of legal knowledge, their desire to enjoy a vacation or meal without conflict, or their unawareness of ombudsmen or authorities capable of resolving disputes amicably before resorting to court. This lack of awareness affected not only guests but also everyone involved in or using services in the hospitality industry.

The supporting evidence for both litigation and mediation, as well as the barriers organizations face at various stages of development, will be explored and summarized, along with proposed questions related to these topics. This approach aims to highlight the decision-making process behind choosing either litigation or mediation for dispute resolution and to uncover the underlying reasons for these choices. It is important to note that some organizations and their employees do not strictly separate these methods and include both clauses in their HR manuals. This can have a deterrent effect due to the costs associated with legal consultancy, such as introduction, updates, changes in advisors, and termination of contractual relationships.

3. *Advantages of Mediation Over Litigation in the Hospitality Industry.*

Since the hotel and restaurant trade are often built on the personal relationships and compatibility of the principals and the employees, businesses in the industry find it essential to handle their disputes in the most efficient, confidential, and personal manner. Litigation is often based on the most unattractive aspects of a party's case. For these reasons, mediation is often the best alternative to litigation.

Disputes in the hospitality industry often centre on business and personal relationships and specific performance issues. Litigation is a blunt tool for trying to solve such problems. Further, disputes between partners or principals of hospitality businesses often involve many contractual arrangements between the parties, as well as complex business relationships.

Control of the Settlement:

The primary advantages of mediation for parties in the hospitality industry can be summarized as follows:

- mediation allows the parties to control the ultimate settlement in a way that is not possible in litigation;
- mediation is relatively inexpensive;
- mediation is non-adversarial;
- mediation is fast;
- mediation usually leads to finality, thereby avoiding the danger of ongoing litigation and negative publicity;
- mediation can provide creative and confidential resolution of disputes.

4. *Conclusion.*

Mediation serves as a vital tool for resolving disputes within the hospitality sector. Within this industry, conflicts often arise between customers and service providers, as well as between local communities and hospitality brands, necessitating mediation for resolution. Crafting tailored solutions relies on a diverse range of disciplines, including negotiation, sociology, political science, anthropology, psychology, law, history, architecture, and archaeological studies. The intricacies of conflicts within the hospitality industry encompass various aspects, ranging from day-to-day operational interactions with consumers to the design and management of visible and hidden aspects of hotels, as well as addressing concerns related to mass tourism and the overall image of tourism destinations. Hosts, companies, organizations, and government entities alike employ hotel industry protocols and empirical procedures to address conflicts and grievances, utilizing data from interviews and surveys to inform mediation efforts concerning issues such as guest complaints, ecological concerns, financial disputes, and social conflicts.

Despite efforts to maintain cordial relationships with customers, employees, local authorities, and the community, legal disputes remain commonplace in the hospitality sector due to the inherently interpersonal and daily nature of the industry's operations. Disputes between staff members, conflicts with neighbouring communities, and legal battles often demand significant attention and resources from management, both in the short and long term. Effective management strategies, such as community planning, relationship management, communication initiatives, and the implementation of conflict prevention and resolution plans, are essential for addressing community grievances and reducing the incidence of legal disputes within the hospitality industry. To establish this, it is crucial to understand the efficiency of mediation, implement strong guidelines that encompass mediation, and educate customers about their rights under mediation.

CHAPTER SEVEN

TECHNIQUES FOR EFFECTIVE MEDIATION

"Empathy is simply listening, holding space, withholding judgment, emotionally connecting, and communicating that incredibly healing message of 'You're not alone.'" — *Brené Brown*

CHAPTER SEVEN: TECHNIQUES FOR EFFECTIVE MEDIATION

1. **Optimizing Mediation Outcomes**

The mediator also needs information on the goals of the parties, the challenges involved, and the restrictions and limitations which plague each party to reach the final conditions of the mediated settlement. The focus of mediation changes as the parties become more aware of their needs and alternative solutions. This perception is necessary to conduct a successful analysis. After communication and factual data have been exchanged and considered by each party, the mediator can then draw upon his/her negotiation skills to improve the parties' positions. What this means is that the focus of mediation may move from solving the problem through solution-finding, to clarifying what is important to each party and why, then devising a way to get the moving party what it wants while protecting the important elements of the other party. This involves jockeying back and forth.

Now, there are some tips, techniques, and general rules to follow which have been identified as being helpful in achieving a successful mediation. The first involves maintaining a productive negotiation atmosphere. It is essential to create an atmosphere which allows parties to express themselves fully, rather than protecting their positions defensively. Second, active listening needs to take place. This would include giving the clients the feeling that they are really understood, not just from the words that are spoken, but also from the emotional content. Third, preparation is a significant factor. Prior to the mediation, the mediator has the opportunity to evaluate the interests of all the parties.

What, then, are the techniques for effective mediation? The process of mediation is divided into five stages to simplify and clarify the direction of the expected output. During the process, particular techniques can help mediators be effective. The stages and their associated techniques and mediator responsibilities are as follows: Setting the Stage, Opening the Process, Listening and Understanding, Validating Options, and Enabling Resolution. These stages are taught at the ADR Center in Italy, where I had the privilege of being a fellow student. This educational center is led by Constantin-Adi Gavrila, President of ADR Center Romania and Senior Expert at ADR Center Global, and Leonardo D'Urso, Co-Founder of ADR Center and Mediator of Complex Disputes. The ADR Center is certified by the International Mediation Institute and qualifies people to be mediation experts; I was one of them.

Parties who want to settle disputes and preserve their relationship often use mediation. Mediation should help parties in dispute settle amicably and cost-efficiently. It is a collaborative and communicative process where both disputants are involved in making decisions; they are not passive as happens in adjudication or arbitration. In mediation, the disputants themselves retain responsibility for the resolution of the dispute. Mediators serve as a catalyst in the structured process by encouraging the disputants to communicate and negotiate, and if needed, use third-party neutral expertise. Many people and organizations have recognized the significant benefits of providing resolution through mediation.

1.1. Definition and Purpose

During mediation, conflicting parties decide for themselves the terms of any settlement, to control their own destinies, and to take responsibility for the results of any agreement. The mediator's responsibility is to provide an environment that enables the disputing parties to develop a self-determined solution that is satisfactory and therefore durable. The value of mediation lies in the control the parties exercise over the process, the outcome, and their own future. For those needing to work together in the future, mediation also allows the restoration of good communication and the development of a foundation for cooperative and respectful future interactions.

In its broadest sense, mediation is a process for resolving disputes or disagreements between two or more parties. Mediation provides the disputing or disagreeing parties an opportunity outside the context of a formal court system to assess their conflicting desires and interests, and to dialogue together, often with the help of a third-party mediator, in order to reach a mutually acceptable and mutually beneficial resolution. The primary purpose of mediation is to explore the common and competing needs and interests of the disputing parties, and to negotiate and reach an agreement that promotes the common good, advances justice, and serves the participants' perceived best interests.

1.2. Benefits and Limitations

Several benefits can be gained from utilizing mediation. These include offering more choices, helping to save time and money, and resolving issues. Utilizing these techniques will provide positive results in reducing conflict. However, when utilizing mediation, one should not be overly optimistic. There are several limitations when using mediation. Some of these limitations include when distrust and dishonesty exist and when one of the disputants is stubborn. It is important to recognize that there are several limitations with the utilization of mediation, especially with trust and dishonesty since a successful resolution is dependent upon developing and sustaining a level of trust between the disputants. As such, the mediator should avoid ignoring the serious problems that the disputants are often unwilling, unendingly, to work out mutual satisfactory outcomes.

The mediator's task is to assist the disputants in exploring and organizing underlying issues for their own understanding. It is important to be able to diagnose the conflict and to know what techniques to use in addressing the issues at hand. There are several techniques that are especially useful in promoting effective communication. These techniques include feedback, active listening, re framing, and restating.

2. **Key Principles of Mediation**

The mediator should contribute to clarifying key issues and areas of common interest; the quality of parties' discussion should aid the crafting of creative and value-maximizing solutions. The mediator should ensure that the final agreement is based on a clear understanding and articulation by the parties of their common interests. The mediator should avoid contributing to the agreement, or otherwise influencing the substance of the settlement. This feature would expose the mediator to accusations of "outcome determination" and would disqualify the mediator from serving another process for resolving irreconcilable differences, including arbitration, should new disputes arise between the parties.

Within this context, the general principles outlined below should be beneficial, if not essential, to effective mediation. The mediator discharges the primary functions of this role by acting as a neutral facilitator, guide, and catalyst. The mediator encourages parties to generate and examine settlement options, and to choose one in the end. The mediator aims to establish and maintain an open and constructive dialogue within which the parties are free to articulate their interests and concerns, thus enabling them to find a solution despite their acrimony, whether it is to resolve a matter completely or narrow the areas of conflict.

The goal of mediation is to achieve a beneficial result for all the participants involved. The mediator helps those involved work together to identify their common goals and promote their interests. Mediation gives those involved in the dispute a real and direct role in deciding the outcome. The mediator does not impose a result on the participants; the participants decide for themselves whether to reach an agreement about bills that are fair and acceptable. A cooperative win-win approach is the foundation of any dispute settlement technique falling within the general process paradigm of problem-solving. This applies to mediation as well.

2.1. Neutrality and Impartiality

The mediator should not give the appearance of being committed to one side but must approach and respond to issues with complete neutrality. The mediator must be seen as truly neutral by both parties. When mediators aim to achieve a social objective rather than focusing on each party's bottom line, they lose their neutrality. While they may develop a trust relationship with clients, they will not be effective mediators. The mediator must avoid allowing their professional experiences or personal values to interfere with their neutrality. A successful mediator is able to separate personal beliefs from their role and maintain control over their behaviour.

The importance of the mediator as a neutral third party cannot be overemphasized. Parties bring their disputes to mediation because they no longer trust each other to act reasonably in resolving the conflict. This lack of trust can result from various factors such as the timing of settlement discussions, damaged relationships, and the inflexibility of one party. For example, in a dispute between a hotel chain and a supplier, the hotel might feel the supplier consistently fails to meet agreed delivery times, while the supplier believes the hotel makes last-minute changes to orders. Both parties might have had several contentious exchanges, leading to a complete breakdown in communication.

When the mediator demonstrates absolute neutrality, the parties transfer their trust from each other to the mediator. Neutrality is fostered when the mediator does not show partiality to either side. A powerful mediator manages the parties by understanding their needs and maintaining a strong, unbiased stance, unaffected by external forces like the environment or internal dynamics such as the parties' relationships. In the hotel-supplier example, the mediator would listen impartially to both sides, understand the core issues, and guide the discussions towards a mutually beneficial resolution without favouring the hotel or the supplier. By doing so, the mediator helps rebuild trust and facilitates a resolution that might have been impossible through direct negotiations between the parties.

Acting neutral is one of the hardest roles a mediator can hold, especially since this neutrality must be maintained over weeks or months. The mediator also has personal and professional obligations, which can add pressure to the mediation process and potentially lead to bias. Thus, mediators must continually practice maintaining neutrality, even in everyday situations such as conflicts at home. This practice helps ensure that neutrality is consistently upheld during mediation sessions. Sometimes, parties may become frustrated by the mediator's neutrality because they seek a quick solution or settlement. This frustration can lead some parties to disrupt the mediation process, ultimately preferring to have their disputes settled by a court. For these parties, neutrality means having a judge decide on their behalf, believing that this represents a fair resolution.

Many parties do not realize that mediation offers them the opportunity to reach a settlement without legal intervention. They perceive a court judgment as neutrality because the judge's decision is final and binding, even if it negatively affects one party. The rigidity of the law means that it often acts impartially rather than neutrally. Legal rulings are based on established statutes and precedents, which do not consider the unique perspectives and needs of the disputing parties. The legislative process enacts laws based on broader societal perspectives, often leading to impartial decisions that may not address the specific context of individual disputes. Thus, while the law aims to be fair and just, its inherent rigidity can result in outcomes that feel impartial rather than truly neutral.

2.2. Confidentiality

Confidentiality in mediation encompasses several key aspects, including the binding nature of agreements reached during the process and the protection of sensitive information shared within the mediation room. Firstly, any agreements made in mediation only become enforceable when they are documented in writing and signed by all involved parties. A mere verbal agreement or handshake holds no legal weight in this context.

Moreover, confidentiality extends to the very fact that mediation is taking place. The participation of disputing parties in mediation cannot be disclosed outside of the mediation process itself, with exceptions typically limited to specific circumstances such as insurance carriers involved in the claim and relevant governmental entities for regulatory purposes.

Furthermore, the mediator's opinions and communications are safeguarded from disclosure. For instance, any statements made by the mediator during court proceedings or to attorneys in preparation for litigation are generally considered prohibited. This protection ensures that parties can freely express their concerns and explore potential solutions without fear of repercussions beyond the mediation room.

Confidentiality requires all parties at the mediation to accept and respect that the discussions, documents produced, and written agreements stemming from the mediation process cannot be revealed to the outside world. This confidentiality is essential in fostering a safe and trusting environment where the mediator and participants can communicate openly and honestly. It promotes the possibility of jointly generated, interest-based outcomes and allows participants to take risks and explore settlement options freely. They can discuss issues and positions candidly, knowing their discussions are not admissible in any legal proceedings without the express consent of the disclosing party.

In the context of courts, confidentiality is often not a factor considered during rulings. In some jurisdictions, parties can request a confidential court session, but it is at the judge's discretion whether to grant it or not based on the sensitivity of the case from the perception of the judge. This lack of confidentiality can leave no room for debate or negotiation with the judge. Family cases, for instance, require confidentiality and respect due to their sensitive nature. In some jurisdictions, particularly those operating under civil law, multiple disputes may be handled simultaneously in the same room, compromising the privacy of sensitive matters. Sometimes, parties may be embarrassed and refrain from providing complete evidence due to societal repercussions.

For example, a woman seeking a divorce might face a prolonged and public court case where known individuals are present, leading to social stigma. Courts sometimes overlook cultural aspects and their impacts, resulting in increased cases and societal scandals. Such situations highlight the necessity of confidentiality in resolving disputes to prevent further conflicts and societal issues.

Thus, in mediation, confidentiality remains a fundamental element. During the listening and understanding stages, the mediator typically reaffirms the confidentiality commitments, even if the parties do not explicitly request it. This practice is part of the ethical standards of mediation, which the mediator upholds throughout the session to ensure a secure and effective resolution process.

3. **Communication Skills for Mediators**

Listening is a communication skill that is of great importance in mediation. Active listening is fundamental to the mediator's ability to understand the agreements and beliefs that disputants hold. It also conveys respect for the issues facing the disputants and conveys understanding of those issues. Empathy builds trust with disputants. It helps establish rapport. In addition, when they know that their feelings or problems are being recognized and understood, individuals are more likely to be open and to display their unmet interests.

Good communication skills are fundamental to effective interaction with parties inside and outside of the mediation setting. Mediators need to be able to communicate effectively with individuals whose backgrounds and communication styles are diverse. Much of the communication that occurs between parties in mediation settings happens through and because of the mediator. The interaction that individuals have with the mediator sets the stage for interactions they have with each other, or conversely, fail to have with each other. The mediator clarifies, reframes, and conveys messages between the disputants, as well as demonstrating his or her understanding, belief, and acceptance of thoughts and feelings expressed by both parties.

3.1. Active Listening

Open-ended, exploratory, and supportive questions are essential in mediation. As mediators guide the parties in using the most effective communication techniques, they need to ask questions that provide additional information about perceptions, feelings, challenges, and consequences. These questions should eventually relate to the future and desired outcomes. Phase one of communication generally focuses on what attracted the parties to each other and what their initial expectations were. During phase two, the different perceptions become more personal and negative. Here, the mediator employs various techniques to explore each party's motivations and expectations of the relationship, facilitating the evaluation of a potential agreement.

Active listening is essential for two primary reasons: it enables the mediator to focus intently on each party's concerns and gradually reduces the risk of misunderstandings, serving as an effective reality check. By actively listening, the mediator ensures that all parties feel heard and understood, which is crucial for fostering trust and cooperation. The mediator should encourage open communication, prompting the parties to share their perspectives and provide feedback to ensure mutual understanding.

For instance, in a mediation between a hotel management company and a franchisee, the mediator might listen carefully to the franchisee's complaints about inadequate marketing support. By asking open-ended questions like, "Can you describe specific instances where you felt the marketing support was lacking?" The mediator encourages detailed responses. This approach not only clarifies the franchisee's concerns but also helps the hotel management company understand the exact issues without feeling attacked.

Furthermore, the mediator can guide the parties to recount events factually, free of emotional details and judgments. This method helps identify the real events, their ideas and perceptions, and potential next steps. For example, instead of saying, "The marketing team never supports us," the franchisee might be encouraged to say, "We requested marketing materials for a local event last month, but they were not provided on time." This factual recounting helps both parties see the situation more clearly and work towards a practical resolution. Overall, active listening not only aids in understanding each party's viewpoint but also paves the way for a constructive dialogue, ultimately leading to a more effective and amicable resolution.

Therefore, active listening is a fundamental skill. It typically comes in the third stage of mediation, after setting the stage and opening the process with the parties. Listening can sometimes lead to more effective problem-solving. Often, people visit a psychiatrist simply to be heard without seeking immediate solutions. Similarly, allowing parties to speak about their case and clarify their situation often leads to a clearer path to settlement. Parties tend to be more stubborn when they feel unheard and when the other party argues against their actions without giving them space to explain. Through active listening, the mediator conducts private and joint meetings, listening repeatedly to the needs and quantifying them for the other party in an effective manner. This demonstrates the mediator's ability to listen, building trust and making the parties feel their case is in capable hands, ultimately leading to a settlement.

On the other hand, in courts, judges often refrain from listening to detailed stories, especially in commercial cases. Nowadays, in some jurisdictions, cases are handled and evaluated virtually after all the dockets of documents have been submitted on time before the case is held. Many litigants believe their case is unique and provide extensive evidence, sometimes translating all documents into the language of the jurisdiction, which is time-consuming. Even with multiple assistants, a judge might struggle to evaluate all these documents thoroughly, as each assistant may interpret them differently. Emotional aspects are often neglected, reducing everything to paperwork. This situation is akin to visiting a doctor who prescribes medication based on common symptoms without listening to the patient's unique experience, such as sleepless nights or fluctuating temperatures. Despite a doctor's expertise, patients often prefer a less renowned doctor who genuinely listens to them. They may also seek out special therapists, life coaches, or alternative medicine solutions simply to be heard. This attentive listening can significantly address their psychological and physiological needs, serving as a major component of their healing process. Thus, reflecting a fundamental human need for being heard and understood.

This analogy underscores the importance of active listening in mediation without being biased towards mediators or courts. While both roles are critical, the ability to listen and provide a space for open communication can make a significant difference in resolving disputes and achieving satisfactory outcomes for all parties involved.

3.2. Empathy and Emotional Intelligence

Proving that one can and does 'walk in the shoes' of the participants can have a powerful effect in showing the participants that the mediator understands and cares enough about their needs and interests to be the impartial facilitator they claim to be. Empathetic gestures are presumed to be genuine and can help build trust. People are more willing to speak up and confront a conflict that is destroying their work and creativity when they feel that they are being heard by the person they ask to help. They are also more open to discussing creative and sometimes offbeat solutions that could have arisen in casual brainstorming sessions, free from the pressures of the formal mediation process. Suspend judgment for the moment; it is the best way to truly understand another's viewpoint.

Empathy is the power that effective mediators possess to stand in the emotional shoes of others and see the situation from their perspective. Empathy is what can make it possible for the mediator to stay connected to the individuals involved, even if the conflict gets 'hot' and a rash reaction is offered. It is also a powerful persuasion technique. As Clement Stone said, "Treat everyone with politeness, even those who are rude to you - not because they are nice, but because you are."

In contrast to the structured environment of court proceedings, where legal formalities often take precedence over personal emotions, mediation offers a unique space for genuine emotional expression and exploration. In court, judges are tasked with adhering to procedural requirements and legal frameworks, which may limit their ability to fully address the emotional nuances of a dispute. This procedural rigidity can often result in outcomes that, while legally sound, fail to address the underlying emotional and relational issues between the parties.

For instance, consider a family law case involving a contentious custody battle. In court, the judge's primary focus is on applying statutory criteria to determine the best interests of the child, often through a purely legal lens. This might involve evaluating factors such as financial stability, living arrangements, and the ability to provide for the child's needs. While these considerations are crucial, the emotional dynamics between the parents, such as feelings of betrayal, guilt, or resentment, are not the primary focus. Consequently, the court's decision, although legally correct, might leave both parties feeling unheard and dissatisfied, potentially exacerbating their conflict.

In contrast, mediation allows for a more holistic approach. In the same custody battle scenario, mediation sessions enable both parents to express their emotions and concerns in a supportive environment. A skilled mediator can help the parents explore the underlying issues that contribute to their conflict, such as communication breakdowns or unmet emotional needs. By addressing these emotional aspects, mediation can foster mutual understanding and cooperation, which is essential for co-parenting. For example, a mother might express her fears about losing her bond with her child, while the father might share his frustrations about being perceived as less capable. Through guided discussions, the mediator can help both parties recognize their common goal: the well-being of their child. This process not only facilitates a more amicable resolution but also lays the groundwork for healthier future interactions.

Critically analyzing the court system, one finds that its inherent limitations in addressing emotional complexities can sometimes lead to adversarial outcomes. In commercial disputes, for example, courts focus on contract terms and legal obligations, often neglecting the relational and emotional dimensions of business partnerships. A court ruling might resolve the contractual issue but leave persistent bitterness and distrust, undermining any potential for future collaboration.

Conversely, mediation provides an opportunity to repair and preserve relationships. In a business partnership dispute, mediation can uncover deeper issues such as miscommunication, unmet expectations, or differing visions for the company's future. By facilitating open dialogue, the mediator can help the partners find common ground and develop a shared plan for moving forward. This not only resolves the immediate dispute but also strengthens the partnership by enhancing communication and trust.

However, mediation is not without its challenges. The success of mediation largely depends on the willingness of the parties to participate in good faith and the skill of the mediator. Unlike court rulings, mediated agreements are voluntary and require mutual consent, which can be difficult to achieve in highly contentious disputes. Furthermore, there is a risk that power imbalances between the parties can affect the fairness of the mediation process, especially if the mediator is not adept at managing such dynamics. While court proceedings are essential for upholding legal principles and providing definitive resolutions, they often fall short in addressing the emotional and relational aspects of disputes. Mediation offers a complementary approach that prioritizes emotional expression and mutual understanding, leading to more holistic and sustainable outcomes. By fostering an environment where parties can openly communicate and address the root causes of their conflict, mediation not only resolves the immediate issue but also promotes healing and collaboration, making it a valuable alternative to traditional litigation.

In mediation, mediators who demonstrate empathy and emotional intelligence create an environment where parties feel safe to share their feelings and concerns openly. This emotional authenticity fosters deeper understanding and paves the way for collaborative problem-solving and resolution. In contrast, the courtroom setting may not always allow for the same level of emotional expression or exploration, as legal proceedings are typically governed by rules of evidence and procedure.

While court judgments are based on legal statutes and precedents, mediation outcomes are shaped by the unique needs, interests, and emotions of the parties involved. By embracing empathy as a cornerstone of mediation practice, mediators can help parties navigate conflicts with compassion, understanding, and dignity, ultimately leading to more satisfying and sustainable resolutions.

4. Conflict Resolution Strategies

Conflict resolution strategies encompass a broad spectrum, from unilateral avoidance and warfare to interest-based negotiation and collaborative problem-solving. The most effective strategy aims at achieving joint gains, where both parties benefit from the resolution. Conflict resolution training should empower participants to embrace unique targeting and integrative agreements, equipping them with techniques to enhance negotiation success.

Various strategies can prevent the escalation of disputes, including interpersonal bargaining, third-party intervention, and ADR. Mediation, a key form of ADR, addresses disruptive conflicts and can significantly enhance group performance. Its integrative approach has proven successful in diverse contexts such as social conflicts, labour disputes, and international trade disagreements. For example, in a labour dispute, mediation can help employers and employees find a mutually acceptable solution that addresses workers' demands while maintaining company productivity. In international trade, mediation can facilitate agreements between countries by focusing on mutual benefits rather than competitive losses.

Conflict resolution training is essential for helping disputants focus on joint gains. Such training involves teaching skills like active listening, empathy, and effective communication. For instance, in a corporate setting, training programs might include role-playing exercises where employees practice negotiating deals that benefit all parties involved. This not only resolves the immediate conflict but also builds a cooperative culture within the organization.

Critical analysis reveals that while interest-based negotiation and mediation are highly effective, their success largely depends on the willingness of parties to engage in good faith. In situations where power imbalances exist, such as a negotiation between a large corporation and a small supplier, the mediator's role becomes crucial in ensuring that the weaker party's interests are adequately represented and protected. Without this, the outcome may still favor the more powerful party, undermining the principle of joint gains.

Furthermore, the effectiveness of these strategies can vary based on cultural contexts. For instance, Western approaches to conflict resolution, which often emphasize direct communication and individual interests, might not be as effective in cultures that prioritize collective well-being and indirect communication. In such cases, conflict resolution training must be tailored to respect and incorporate cultural differences, ensuring that the techniques taught are relevant and effective in the given context.

In conflict resolution, parties often find satisfaction through making concessions and sacrifices. Sacrifice is an integral part of human conflict resolution, exemplified by instances where individuals relinquish long-held positions for better prospects elsewhere. Personal conflict resolution hinges on the willingness of parties to make sacrifices, leading to a final settlement based on mutual agreement.

Contrastingly, court decisions lack the same neutrality and impartiality found in personal conflict resolution. Court rulings may favor one party over the other, triggering feelings of jealousy and injustice. Rather than prioritizing resolution, court decisions often serve as mandates, potentially exacerbating conflicts instead of resolving them.

Conflict resolution extends far beyond courtroom proceedings, particularly in maintaining business continuity and fostering mutually beneficial outcomes. In commercial and civil disputes, achieving a win-win scenario is often facilitated by mediation. This approach offers parties the opportunity for amicable resolution, potentially even restoring their relationship as business partners.

For example, consider a dispute between two business partners over the distribution of profits. Rather than resorting to litigation, mediation allows the partners to engage in constructive dialogue, exploring various solutions that accommodate both parties' interests. Through mediation, they may reach a compromise that not only resolves the immediate conflict but also strengthens their business relationship moving forward.

Conflict resolution extends beyond court decisions; it aims to satisfy both parties and maintain business continuity. Achieving a win-win scenario, especially in commercial and civil disputes, is facilitated by mediation. This approach provides parties with the opportunity for amicable resolution, potentially even restoring them as partners. Ultimately, mediation offers the best outcome for cases where parties seek mutually beneficial solutions.

4.1. *Interest-Based Bargaining*

Interest-based bargaining is a negotiation approach that focuses on identifying and addressing the underlying interests, needs, desires, concerns, and fears of the parties involved. Unlike traditional bargaining methods that may prioritize positional stances or power dynamics, interest-based bargaining seeks to find mutually beneficial solutions by understanding what each party truly wants and why. It emphasizes collaboration, open communication, and creative problem-solving to reach agreements that satisfy the core interests of all parties.

When applied in mediation, interest-based bargaining takes on a facilitative role, with a mediator guiding the parties through the process of exploring their interests and finding common ground. Mediation provides a confidential and flexible environment where parties can freely discuss their needs and concerns without the adversarial atmosphere often present in court proceedings. The mediator helps parties communicate effectively, generate options, and evaluate potential solutions, with the goal of reaching a mutually acceptable agreement.

In contrast to interest-based bargaining in mediation, court proceedings typically adhere to an adversarial model. Here, parties present their cases based on legal arguments and evidence, and a judge renders a decision based on applicable laws and precedents. While court decisions can bring resolution to the immediate dispute, they often fail to address the underlying interests driving the conflict. This can leave one or both parties feeling dissatisfied or resentful, as their deeper concerns may remain unacknowledged or unresolved.

For example, in a civil dispute over property ownership, the court may rule in favour of one party based on legal ownership documents without considering the emotional attachment or financial investment of the other party. This narrow focus on legalities can lead to outcomes that overlook the parties' underlying interests, resulting in lingering dissatisfaction and strained relationships.

Furthermore, court processes are notorious for their lengthiness, expense, and emotional toll. Legal proceedings can drag on for months or even years, consuming valuable time and resources for all involved. The adversarial nature of court litigation often exacerbates tensions between parties, leading to heightened stress and emotional strain. Additionally, the financial costs associated with legal representation and court fees can be substantial, placing further burdens on individuals already grappling with the conflict.

Overall, while court proceedings may offer a resolution to disputes, they often fall short in addressing the underlying interests of the parties and can impose significant practical and emotional burdens on all involved.

The implications of interest-based bargaining in both mediation and court are significant. In mediation, parties can actively participate in crafting solutions that meet their unique needs and interests. They retain control over the outcome and are more likely to comply with agreements reached through a collaborative process. Additionally, mediation can preserve or even improve relationships between parties, making it particularly beneficial in ongoing or future interactions.

On the other hand, in court, the focus is primarily on legal rights and obligations rather than the underlying interests of the parties. While court decisions may provide a resolution to the immediate dispute, they often do not address the root causes of conflict and may fail to fully satisfy the parties involved. Moreover, court rulings are binding and may exacerbate tensions between parties, making future cooperation more challenging.

Overall, mediation offers a more holistic and constructive approach to resolving disputes by prioritizing the interests and needs of the parties involved. By fostering open communication, collaboration, and creative problem-solving, mediation can lead to more satisfactory outcomes and preserve relationships, making it a preferable option for many parties seeking resolution outside of the courtroom.

4.2. Brainstorming

Generally, it is best to use a well-defined model in helping dissect the problem, with emphasis on defining and clarifying what you need to fix about the problem. Once you are both confident that you understand the problem intellectually, then you need to focus on a solution. Brainstorming is generally an area that you may require some practice at. In brainstorming, the idea is quantity, not quality. If you have a number of people involved in the brainstorming, they all need paper and pencil. It is generally best to have people standing up so that they don't get too relaxed. Write down every idea, no matter how "wacky". This gives a wide selection of ideas, which widens your range of potential solutions. Brainstorming is for developing problem solutions and strategies. It is a useful creativity exercise as well.

When people are engaged in conflict, they spend a lot of energy criticizing and refuting each other's ideas. This creates tension and frustration. When they are asked to develop solutions, it is hard for them to change the habit of negative confrontation and/or competitive reasoning. As a mediator, you can help them to shift their attention from the problem to the solution by incorporating some kind of activity that supports the development of solutions. One of the modules mentioned earlier, the negotiation module, spoke about integrating problem solving and negotiation techniques. Without going into problem solving in a lot of detail here.

Brainstorming in a courtroom setting is rare. Court proceedings follow a formal, adversarial structure where legal arguments and evidence are presented to a judge or jury. The focus is on proving one party's case over the other, rather than collaboratively generating solutions. While judges may consider various legal arguments and precedents, the emphasis is on applying existing laws rather than generating new ideas or options.

In legal proceedings such as civil litigation, brainstorming is seldom practiced due to the formal and adversarial nature of court processes. Unlike mediation or negotiation sessions where parties are encouraged to collaborate and explore creative solutions, courtrooms operate within a structured framework where legal arguments and evidence are presented to a judge or jury.

For instance, in a civil dispute over contractual obligations between two business entities, each party presents its case by outlining contractual terms, relevant facts, and legal arguments to support its position. The focus is on persuading the judge or jury of the validity of their interpretation of the contract and the associated legal rights and obligations.

However, the courtroom environment, with its emphasis on procedural rules and adherence to legal precedent, often limits the scope for brainstorming or collaborative problem-solving. Instead, lawyers advocate for their clients' interests through formalized procedures, such as presenting evidence, examining witnesses, and making legal arguments. The goal is to convince the court of the merits of their case based on existing laws and legal interpretations.

Moreover, judges in courtrooms typically base their decisions on established legal principles and precedents, prioritizing consistency and predictability in judicial rulings. While they may consider various legal arguments presented by the parties, the primary focus remains on applying existing laws rather than generating new ideas or options.

This adherence to legal precedent ensures fairness and impartiality in judicial decision-making but may limit the exploration of innovative or alternative approaches to dispute resolution. As a result, while court proceedings offer a formal mechanism for resolving legal disputes, they may not always provide the flexibility or creativity necessary to address complex issues effectively.

The implications of brainstorming in mediation versus the court are significant. In mediation, the collaborative nature of brainstorming encourages parties to actively participate in finding solutions that meet their interests and needs. It promotes open communication and cooperation, leading to more satisfactory outcomes and potentially preserving or even improving relationships between parties. By contrast, the adversarial nature of court proceedings may exacerbate tensions between parties and lead to win-lose outcomes, where one party prevails at the expense of the other.

5. **Cultural Sensitivity in Mediation**

What may seem appropriate behaviour or communication to one person may be disappointing or insulting to another. Understanding and showing sensitivity to the cultural context in which disputes arise is crucial. Each individual's perspective must be considered, and the mediator should avoid stereotyping based on cultural or social identity. Recognizing that people often act, react, and perceive the world differently due to their cultural backgrounds can help the mediator overcome a significant obstacle to effective communication between disputants.

For example, in a business dispute between a Japanese company and an American company, the cultural differences in communication styles can be stark. Japanese business culture often values indirect communication, where context and non-verbal cues play a significant role. In contrast, American business culture typically favors direct and explicit communication. A Japanese executive might interpret an American's straightforward approach as rude or aggressive, while the American might view the Japanese executive's indirectness as evasive or unclear.

In such cases, the mediator's role is to bridge this cultural gap by gaining the trust and understanding of both parties with cultural sensitivity. This involves actively listening to each party and acknowledging their cultural norms and communication styles. Instead of generalizing responses based on cultural stereotypes, the mediator should encourage each party to share information about their specific situation. This helps in identifying and resolving potential communication barriers.

For instance, if the Japanese executive is hesitant to directly express disagreement due to cultural norms, the mediator can facilitate the conversation by creating a safe environment where indirect feedback is valued and understood. Similarly, the mediator can help the American executive appreciate the subtleties of non-verbal communication and the importance of reading between the lines in Japanese culture.

In another scenario, consider a family dispute involving members from different cultural backgrounds, such as a mixed marriage between a Hispanic and a European family. In Hispanic culture, family loyalty and collective decision-making are often paramount, whereas European cultures might emphasize individualism and personal autonomy. In resolving conflicts, the mediator must be sensitive to these cultural values and norms.

The mediator should facilitate discussions where each party explains their cultural perspectives on family roles and decision-making. For example, the Hispanic family member might feel disrespected if decisions are made without family consensus, while the European family member might feel their independence is being undermined. Understanding these cultural contexts allows the mediator to propose solutions that respect both family traditions and individual preferences. It's evident that cultural sensitivity in mediation not only fosters effective communication but also builds trust and rapport between parties. However, mediators must be cautious not to overemphasize cultural differences to the point of reinforcing stereotypes. Instead, they should focus on understanding the unique cultural dynamics at play and use this understanding to facilitate a more nuanced and empathetic dialogue.

Ultimately, being aware that people act, react, and perceive the world differently because of their cultural backgrounds can transform potential misunderstandings into opportunities for deeper connection and resolution. By addressing cultural nuances thoughtfully, mediators can help parties navigate their differences and arrive at mutually satisfying agreements.

5.1. Understanding Cultural Differences

Culturally appropriate ways of formulating questions, understanding both spoken and unspoken communication, observing parties' usage of cultural idioms or metaphors, noting hearing styles, amount of eye contact, space considerations, and cultural behaviours before, during, and after mediation are crucial in avoiding misunderstandings and ensuring smooth interactions. Mediators trained in cultures outside their own are better equipped to assist parties and provide more effective service. Interaction between individual cultures is essential, and mediation exemplifies such interaction. The greater the mediator's sensitivity in dealing with the culture of the disputing parties, the more constructive the mediation process will be.

Effective communication is integral to successful mediation. Establishing rapport with parties from different backgrounds, beliefs, and values requires the mediator to have a deep understanding of those parties. However, this can be challenging since many people have an incomplete understanding of their own culture, let alone others. To better understand cultural differences, mediators must remain flexible, open to cultural issues, and willing to change their attitudes and beliefs. It is vital for mediators not to judge any culture. Cultural differences can be leveraged as strengths within mediation, fostering more effective conflict resolution. Understanding culture is also crucial when handling disputes involving married couples or intimate partners.

Understanding cultural differences involves recognizing and respecting the diverse beliefs, values, customs, communication styles, and behaviors of individuals from different cultural backgrounds. This includes aspects such as language, body language, social norms, traditions, and religious practices. In mediation, understanding cultural differences is crucial for creating an inclusive and effective process that addresses the needs and concerns of all parties involved.

Example in Practice

Consider a mediation involving a dispute between a Latino family-owned business and a corporate client from the United States. In Latino culture, family and respect for elders are paramount. During mediation, the Latino family members may rely heavily on the input and guidance of the family patriarch. The mediator must recognize this dynamic and ensure that the patriarch's views are respected and considered throughout the process.

In contrast, the American corporate client might prioritize efficiency and direct communication, expecting a swift and straightforward negotiation process. The mediator needs to balance these differing expectations by facilitating a respectful dialogue that honours the Latino family's cultural values while also addressing the corporate client's desire for efficiency. This might involve structuring the mediation sessions to allow for family discussions and decision-making processes, ensuring that the corporate client understands and respects this approach.

Critical Analysis of Mediation vs. Courtroom

In a courtroom setting, such cultural nuances are often overlooked. Court proceedings follow a formal, standardized framework that prioritizes legal arguments and evidence over the personal and cultural context of the parties involved. For instance, if the same dispute were resolved in court, the judge might not have the flexibility to accommodate the Latino family's decision-making process. The emphasis would be on legal documentation and precedent, potentially marginalizing the cultural values that are central to the Latino family. This could lead to feelings of alienation and dissatisfaction among the Latino family members, who might perceive the process as disrespectful to their cultural norms.

Implications for Mediation and Courtroom Processes

The implications of understanding cultural differences in mediation versus the court are significant. In mediation, parties can actively participate in shaping the resolution process in a culturally sensitive manner. Mediators can tailor their approach to accommodate diverse cultural perspectives, fostering an environment of inclusivity and mutual respect. This can lead to more sustainable and satisfactory resolutions that preserve relationships and promote understanding between parties.

On the other hand, in the court system, the lack of attention to cultural differences may contribute to feelings of alienation and dissatisfaction, particularly among parties from marginalized or minority backgrounds. Court decisions may not fully address the underlying cultural factors at play, leading to outcomes that do not meet the needs or expectations of the parties involved.

In conclusion, culturally sensitive mediation recognizes and respects the diverse backgrounds of disputants, facilitating effective communication and mutual understanding. Mediators must be adept at navigating cultural nuances to help parties find common ground and resolve disputes amicably. This approach not only leads to better outcomes for the parties involved but also promotes a more inclusive and respectful dispute resolution process. In contrast, the rigid structure of courtroom proceedings often fails to accommodate cultural diversity, resulting in less satisfactory outcomes and potentially exacerbating conflicts. Therefore, promoting cultural sensitivity in mediation is essential for achieving fair and lasting resolutions.

5.2. Avoiding Cultural Misunderstandings

Cultural unawareness or disrespect can leave lasting impressions. When these conflicts arise, the mediator should take rational steps toward understanding and addressing the root sources and the more visible symptoms of the misunderstanding. To avoid cultural misunderstandings, the mediator should always be well prepared and research the parties and people involved before attempting to set up a meeting. Scheduling conflicts often arise from cultural considerations, and the conflict will sour before it even begins if, for example, an observant Muslim learns that an inclusive meeting falls on the Friday Sabbath or a Hindu discovers that the timing shows disrespect for a religious holiday.

Cultural misunderstandings can pose a great challenge to the mediator, not only potentially interfering with effective communication but also potentially forming a serious conflict in and of themselves. In multilateral disputes particularly, some representatives carry with them feelings, convictions, and ideas that stem primarily, and sometimes exclusively, from their culture. Religious and official holidays, social customs, and traditions are examples of cultural facets of international negotiations that need to be carefully attended to.

Avoiding Cultural Misunderstandings involves recognizing and respecting the cultural differences and sensitivities of all parties involved in a conflict resolution process. This includes understanding cultural norms, beliefs, values, communication styles, and traditions to prevent potential conflicts and ensure effective communication and collaboration.

In mediation, avoiding cultural misunderstandings is essential for creating a supportive and inclusive environment where parties feel respected and understood. Mediators must be proactive in researching the cultural backgrounds of the parties involved and taking steps to accommodate cultural considerations. Imagine a mediator scheduling a meeting without considering cultural holidays. For instance, setting a meeting on a Friday during Friday-prayers for a Muslim or during a Hindu religious holiday could cause tension before the discussion even begins. So, before arranging any meetings, it's vital for the mediator to research the cultural backgrounds of the parties involved and plan accordingly. Failure to do so can lead to miscommunication, tension, and breakdowns in the mediation process, ultimately hindering the resolution of the conflict.

In contrast, the courtroom setting may not prioritize cultural considerations to the same extent. Court proceedings often follow rigid procedural rules and may not adequately address the cultural needs or sensitivities of the parties involved. This can lead to misunderstandings or conflicts arising from cultural differences being overlooked or misunderstood by legal professionals and court personnel.

The implications of avoiding cultural misunderstandings differ between mediation and the court. In mediation, effectively addressing cultural differences can lead to more successful outcomes by fostering understanding, cooperation, and trust between parties. By accommodating cultural considerations and respecting diverse perspectives, mediators can help parties navigate cultural differences constructively, leading to more sustainable and mutually satisfactory resolutions.

On the other hand, in the court system, cultural misunderstandings may impair tensions between parties and hinder the resolution process. Legal professionals may lack the cultural awareness or sensitivity needed to effectively address cultural differences, potentially leading to biased or insensitive treatment of parties from diverse backgrounds. This can result in feelings of downgrading, injustice, and dissatisfaction among parties, ultimately undermining the credibility and fairness of the legal process.

6. **Power Imbalance and Fairness**

Effect of power imbalance on mediation: In a communication imbalance, it can damage the effectiveness of both the content and the process of conflict resolution. The powerful party dominates the discussion, almost ignoring the weaker party's interests and placing less value on the settlement result. A properly functioning mediation process is one of fairness, first by offering a comfortable and empowering environment for participation, even with limited power, and second by helping to level the relative power of the disputants. Power imbalance results in satisfying only the stronger party's interests. Further consequences could occur, such as social value, political issues, or the weaker party's identity. The needs and concerns of the weaker party should not be ignored.

Identifying the power imbalance: Understanding the nature of formal and informal sources of power, such as age, race, gender, physical attractiveness, democracy, wealth, education, status, and one's grasp of power. It is important to know why the parties have been left in a state of power imbalance and what legal, financial, physical, mental, personnel, and HRs are pertinent to resolve the dispute.

In mediation, power imbalances can significantly impact the fairness and effectiveness of conflict resolution processes. For instance, consider a scenario where one party holds more social status, wealth, or authority than the other. In such cases, the powerful party might dominate discussions, ignoring the interests of the weaker party and prioritizing their own goals. This imbalance can lead to an unfair settlement that disregards the needs and concerns of the less powerful party.

In contrast, within the court system, power imbalances may not always be adequately addressed. Legal proceedings often prioritize legal rights and precedents, potentially overlooking the underlying power dynamics at play. As a result, court decisions may favour the more powerful party, reinforcing existing inequalities and perceptions of unfairness.

However, in mediation, a skilled mediator can identify and address power imbalances to promote fairness and equality. By creating a supportive and empowering environment, the mediator can ensure that all parties have the opportunity to voice their concerns and interests. Additionally, the mediator can employ techniques to level the relative power of the disputants, such as active listening, reframing, and reality testing.

For example, the Maasai people, living in Kenya and Tanzania, are known for their cattle herding and distinctive culture. Household disputes among the Maasai often revolve around issues related to land and property, particularly cattle and land ownership. These disputes can stem from disagreements over inheritance, grazing rights, or land boundaries. In Maasai culture, there can be a gender and age imbalance, where certain roles or assets are traditionally designated for men or women. For example, the ownership and management of cattle may be primarily the domain of men, while women may have more influence over household affairs. These disputes can sometimes lead to tensions within families or between community members and may require mediation or traditional conflict resolution methods to reach a resolution.

Resolving household disputes among the Maasai through courts may not always be the most effective or culturally appropriate approach. Maasai culture places significant emphasis on customary laws and traditional dispute resolution mechanisms, which are deeply rooted in their cultural values and practices. These disputes often involve complex social dynamics and customary norms that may not align with formal legal systems. Additionally, courts may lack the understanding of Maasai customs and traditions necessary to reach a fair and satisfactory resolution. Therefore, attempting to solve these disputes solely through courts may overlook important cultural considerations and may not lead to outcomes that are perceived as fair or just by the Maasai community. Overall, mediation offers a more flexible and inclusive approach to addressing power imbalances, allowing for a fairer and more equitable resolution of conflicts compared to court proceedings. By prioritizing the needs and concerns of all parties involved, mediation can help restore balance and promote social justice within diverse cultural contexts.

6.1. Addressing Power Dynamics

Addressing power dynamics in mediation involves recognizing and addressing disparities in influence, control, and resources between parties involved in a dispute. In family law and workplace situations, power imbalances can be particularly significant, with one party often having more power or feeling more empowered than the other. In such cases, a mediator can level the playing field by conducting separate pre-mediation sessions with each party to understand their perspectives, concerns, and the degree of power imbalance. This helps the mediator develop strategies to ensure that the mediation process is fair and that both parties have an equal voice.

In family law, power imbalances often arise, especially in cases of domestic violence or financial dependency. For instance, in a divorce mediation where one spouse has been the primary breadwinner and the other has been financially dependent, the financially dominant spouse may exert undue influence over the decisions. Mediators can address this by meeting with the financially weaker party before the first joint session to ensure they do not feel pressured to make decisions against their interests. This pre-session also allows the mediator to assess the true extent of the power imbalance and plan accordingly.

Example: Addressing Power Imbalance in Divorce Mediation

Consider a scenario where a wife, who has been a homemaker for many years, is mediating a divorce settlement with her husband, who has been the sole earner. The husband might feel more empowered due to his control over the family finances. The mediator, recognizing this imbalance, might choose to meet with the wife separately to discuss her concerns and ensure she understands her rights and the mediation process. The mediator could also provide resources or suggest consulting with a financial advisor to help the wife feel more informed and confident.

During the joint mediation sessions, the mediator would employ techniques to ensure that the husband's financial control does not dominate the discussions. For example, they might set ground rules that prevent one party from interrupting the other, or they could use reality testing to gently challenge the husband's assumptions and ensure the wife's needs and perspectives are considered equally. This approach helps create a more balanced negotiation environment, increasing the likelihood of a fair and mutually acceptable agreement.

Example: Balancing Power in Workplace Mediation

In a workplace mediation involving a conflict between a manager and an employee, the manager's position of authority can create a significant power imbalance. The mediator can address this by initially meeting with the employee in a private session to understand their concerns and help them articulate their issues without fear of retaliation. The mediator might also coach the employee on effective communication strategies and ensure that they feel comfortable and safe during the mediation process.

In the joint sessions, the mediator can structure the discussions to ensure that the employee has equal opportunities to speak, and that the manager does not dominate the conversation. Techniques such as using a round-robin method, where each party speaks in turn without interruption, brainstorming ideas that can be effective towards their work relationship. The mediator can also provide summaries and reflections to validate the employee's points and ensure they are heard and considered.

Power dynamics are a crucial consideration in mediation, as they can significantly impact the fairness and outcomes of the process. Effective mediators are adept at identifying and mitigating these imbalances to create an equitable environment. However, the challenge lies in the subtleties of power dynamics that are not always overt. For example, cultural or gender-based power imbalances may not be immediately apparent but can still influence the mediation process. Mediators must be trained to recognize these nuances and employ strategies that address both visible and hidden power disparities.

In contrast to mediation, court proceedings often fail to adequately address power imbalances. The formal and adversarial nature of the court system inherently favours those who can afford better legal representation, thus impairing existing power disparities. For instance, in a workplace harassment case, an employee might face an intimidating court process against a well-resourced employer, potentially leading to an unjust outcome due to the imbalance in legal expertise and financial resources.

Addressing power dynamics in mediation is essential for ensuring a fair and effective dispute resolution process. By recognizing and proactively managing power imbalances, mediators can help create a more balanced negotiation environment, empowering all parties to participate fully and reach mutually beneficial agreements. The examples of divorce and workplace mediations illustrate how tailored approaches can mitigate power disparities and promote equitable outcomes. In comparison, the court system's limitations in addressing power imbalances highlight the advantages of mediation in providing a more inclusive and fair resolution process.

6.2 *Ensuring Fairness*

The importance of fairness in the mediation process itself cannot be understated, the mediation process provides a more supportive and less intimidating environment, crucial for parties anxious or uncertain about their ability to succeed in court. This sense of security is particularly important for those less confident, as they need reassurance and a fair opportunity to present their views before reaching a settlement.

However, fairness is not always guaranteed in mediation. There is a risk that one party may not adequately represent their case or fully understand its implications. This can undermine their confidence in achieving a favourable outcome if the case were to go to court. For instance, in family law, a spouse may feel pressured to accept terms that are not in their best interest due to the mediator's influence or the other spouse's tactics, particularly in cases involving a history of domestic violence. In such scenarios, mediators must be proactive, ensuring that each spouse feels safe and that decisions are not made out of fear of dominance.

Consider a scenario where a hotel owner disputes a management company's performance under their management agreement. The owner might feel that the company has not met the agreed-upon standards for maintaining the hotel's quality and profitability. During mediation, the owner may lack the detailed financial knowledge or operational expertise that the management company's representatives possess. The mediator's role becomes crucial in ensuring that the owner's concerns are fairly heard and addressed, preventing the management company from leveraging their superior knowledge to push through an unfavourable settlement.

Similarly, a hotel owner operating under a franchise agreement might feel that the franchisor is not providing the promised support or is imposing unfair fees. In mediation, the franchisor, often a large corporation with significant legal resources, might dominate the discussions. The mediator must ensure that the hotel owner has equal opportunity to present their case and that the power imbalance does not lead to a one-sided settlement. Providing the owner with access to independent legal or financial advice can help level the playing field.

For example, consider a situation where a couple is mediating their divorce settlement. The husband might be a high-earning professional with access to a team of lawyers, while the wife might be a stay-at-home parent with limited financial resources and legal knowledge. In this scenario, the mediator would meet with the wife first, helping her to articulate her needs and concerns, such as securing adequate spousal support and child custody arrangements. During this private session, the mediator can also provide her with information about her legal rights and options, empowering her to participate more effectively in the mediation process. Another strategy involves the mediator guiding the couple towards focusing on their shared interests and long-term goals, rather than getting bogged down in positional bargaining. For instance, in the context of negotiating child custody, the mediator can help the parents concentrate on the best interests of the child, rather than using the child as a bargaining chip. By reframing the discussion around mutual goals, the mediator can help reduce the impact of power imbalances and facilitate a more collaborative and constructive negotiation process.

The principle of procedural fairness in mediation is vital for several reasons. Firstly, it ensures that both parties have an equal opportunity to present their case and negotiate terms without undue pressure. This is particularly important in cases where there is a significant power imbalance, as it helps level the playing field and prevent one party from taking advantage of the other. Secondly, procedural fairness helps maintain the integrity of the mediation process. If parties perceive the process as biased or unfair, they are less likely to accept the outcome and more likely to seek alternative means of resolving the dispute, such as litigation. This can lead to increased costs, time, and emotional stress for both parties.

In contrast, court proceedings often struggle with issues of fairness due to their adversarial nature and the inherent power imbalances that can arise from differences in legal representation and resources. For example, in a civil lawsuit between a hotel owner and a large management company, the company's ability to hire a team of experienced lawyers can significantly overshadow the owner's capacity to argue their case, leading to a perception of unfairness and potentially unjust outcomes. Similarly, in family law cases, the adversarial nature of court proceedings can impair conflicts, leaving one or both parties feeling dissatisfied or resentful.

6.3 *Ethical Considerations in Mediation*

The primary function of ethics within mediation is to promote trust, treat parties with respect, and recognize that the parties are the primary participants. The mediator's role is to facilitate communication and assist in achieving an appropriate and acceptable agreement without favouring any individual party or coercing agreement in any way. This ethical responsibility is crucial because the quality and service of mediators are largely unobservable by those they serve. Consequently, there is little consumer protection in the traditional sense, making it imperative that mediators adhere to high ethical standards to ensure fairness and trust in the process. By protecting the details of the mediation, parties are encouraged to communicate openly and honestly, which is essential for reaching a resolution. Ethical considerations in mediation aim to create an environment where parties can freely share their thoughts without fear of coercion or bias. This principle is critical in all mediation contexts, whether in family law, hotel management agreements, workplace disputes, or restaurant conflicts.

In the context of hotel management agreements, the ethical responsibility of the mediator is particularly significant. For example, consider a dispute between a hotel owner and a management company over the terms of their contract. The owner may feel that the management company has not met performance standards, while the management company might argue that the owner has not provided adequate resources. In such a case, the mediator must ensure that both parties feel heard and respected, fostering an environment where they can discuss their concerns openly. By maintaining confidentiality and impartiality, the mediator can help the parties explore potential solutions without the fear that their words will be used against them outside the mediation room. This approach can lead to a mutually beneficial resolution, such as renegotiating certain terms of the contract or establishing clearer performance metrics. The ethical conduct of the mediator in this scenario is paramount; by adhering to high ethical standards, the mediator helps build trust between the parties, making it more likely that they will commit to the agreed-upon solution. This trust is crucial because it encourages ongoing cooperation and reduces the likelihood of future disputes.

In workplace disputes, the role of ethics in mediation is equally vital. Imagine a situation where an employee feels discriminated against by their employer. The power imbalance between the employer and employee can make it difficult for the employee to voice their concerns. A mediator must address this power disparity by creating a safe space for the employee to express their feelings and ensuring that the employer listens without interruption. By doing so, the mediator can facilitate a constructive dialogue that focuses on finding a resolution that respects the employee's rights while addressing the employer's concerns. This might involve implementing new workplace policies, providing training for management, or offering a fair settlement to the employee. The ethical approach in such mediation helps prevent the employee from feeling marginalized and ensures that the employer takes the concerns seriously, promoting a healthier workplace environment.

Despite the importance of ethical standards in mediation, the same level of scrutiny and accountability may not always be applied in court proceedings. In contrast to mediation, where the mediator's ethical conduct is paramount to the process, court ethics may vary depending on the judge, legal jurisdiction, and prevailing legal norms. While courts are bound by legal precedent and procedural rules, the ethical standards governing judicial conduct may not always align with those of mediation. This disconnect highlights the unique role that ethics play in mediation, where the mediator's commitment to fairness, impartiality, and confidentiality is essential to ensuring trust and integrity in the process.

For instance, in a courtroom, a judge is required to adhere to strict procedural rules and legal precedents, which might not always allow for the same level of individualized attention and sensitivity to the parties' needs as mediation. A judge's primary role is to apply the law impartially, which can sometimes result in one party feeling disadvantaged or misunderstood, particularly in complex disputes where emotional and relational dynamics play a significant role. In contrast, mediators can take a more flexible approach, tailoring the process to the specific needs and cultural contexts of the parties involved. This flexibility can be especially important in resolving disputes in culturally diverse settings, such as international hotel management agreements or workplaces with a multicultural workforce.

Overall, the ethical considerations in mediation serve to create a more inclusive, respectful, and effective process for resolving disputes. By promoting trust, confidentiality, and impartiality, mediators can help parties navigate their conflicts in a way that courts may not always be able to, ultimately leading to more satisfactory and sustainable outcomes. In hotel management agreements, ethical mediation ensures that both owners and management companies can resolve disputes in a manner that supports ongoing collaboration and operational success. In workplace disputes, ethical mediation fosters a healthier work environment by addressing power imbalances and ensuring fair treatment for all employees. And in family law, ethical mediation protects vulnerable parties, ensuring that resolutions are fair and not coerced, thus promoting long-term stability and harmony.

6.4 *Conflict of Interest*

Conflict of interest is a critical aspect of mediation ethics, and it is essential for mediators to manage it carefully to maintain the trust and integrity of the mediation process. Mediators must be vigilant about their own potential biases and connections to the dispute or the parties involved. It is up to the individual mediator to determine whether they can remain impartial and effectively manage the mediation. Codes of ethics introduced by the sector or professional organizations often lay down specific rules and processes to address conflicts of interest, ensuring that mediators adhere to high standards of conduct.

One fundamental tool for managing conflicts of interest is the Confidentiality Agreement With a Mediator Model. This agreement ensures that all parties understand the mediator's role and the bounds of confidentiality. It raises critical questions: How is this presented? How binding is the relationship? Who can examine the details of the dispute? Does a mediator make detailed notes? Who can have access to these notes? How are these matters handled within the institutions or organizations that may influence the dispute?

The mediator should never act as a neutral party in disputes that involve him personally or that relate to his own situation. If a mediator finds himself in such a position, he must refuse to mediate the conflict to avoid any appearance of bias. For example, in a dispute involving hotel management agreements, if the mediator has a financial interest in one of the hotels or a personal relationship with one of the parties, he should immediately recuse himself from the case. Failure to do so could lead to a perceived or real conflict of interest, undermining the fairness of the process. If a conflict of interest is imminent and the mediator becomes aware of it ahead of time, he should refuse the mandate as soon as he is aware of the real situation. For instance, if a mediator is asked to mediate a workplace dispute in a restaurant where he previously worked or has close ties with the management, he should disclose this connection and decline to mediate. This pre-emptive action helps maintain transparency and trust in the mediation process.

In cases where a compromise that satisfies one party does not fully address the needs of both parties, the mediator should ensure full transparency. He should recognize the suspicion of a possible conflict of interest and take appropriate steps, including making a written disclosure to lay matters out to the parties beforehand. This disclosure can confirm the mediator's impartiality and commitment to a fair process.

For example, in an employment dispute between a restaurant employee and employer, the mediator should disclose any prior relationships or interests that might influence his neutrality. A written confidentiality agreement should be established to assure both parties that the content of discussions remains confidential, and that the mediator will not retain any information that could be used against them in future proceedings. Some mediators sign a declaration that the content of discussions is confidential, reinforcing their commitment to impartiality and the ethical handling of information. Others may prefer not to retain the information and instead write a confidentiality agreement with the parties. This agreement ensures that all details shared during mediation remain private and are not disclosed without consent.

Unlike mediation, which emphasizes ethical conduct and conflict of interest management, court proceedings may sometimes overlook these critical aspects. Judges are expected to recuse themselves from cases where there is a conflict of interest, but the reality is that bias can occasionally influence their decisions. For instance, Judge Kreep's judicial conduct was marred by instances reflecting bias involving ethnicity, nationality, race, gender, and sexual orientation, as evidenced in cases reviewed by the Commission on Judicial Performance and Supreme Court cases. His remarks included inappropriate comments about an attorney's accent and nationality, suggesting deportation based on these factors. Additionally, during a sidebar in a prostitution case, he made a racially insensitive remark about "Chinese prostitutes," followed by a dismissive comment with "No offense to Chinese people." Judge Kreep also frequently addressed individuals with Hispanic surnames in Spanish without their consent, perpetuating stereotypes and potentially undermining their professional status in the courtroom. These actions collectively raised significant concerns about Judge Kreep's ability to uphold judicial decorum, fairness, and respect for diversity within the legal system.[30]

In summary, mediators must adhere to strict ethical standards to manage conflicts of interest effectively. By doing so, they promote trust, treat parties with respect, and ensure that the mediation process remains fair and unbiased. Whether dealing with disputes in restaurants, hotels, or workplaces, the mediator's commitment to impartiality, confidentiality, and transparency is crucial for a successful and equitable resolution. This ethical responsibility contrasts with the more varied application of ethical frameworks in court proceedings, highlighting the unique and essential role of ethics in mediation.

7 Technology and Mediation

7.1 *The rise of Online Dispute Resolution (ODR)*

The rise of ODR, accelerated by the COVID-19 pandemic, has prompted legal professionals and mediators to critically assess the security of using popular online conferencing platforms such as Zoom, and the need for enhanced security measures across different platforms. The surge in e-mediation, driven largely by the pandemic's restrictions, has underscored the importance of secure communication channels in conflict resolution. Yet, concerns persist among participants about the safety of their data when using teleconferencing services like Zoom, WebEx, and Skype for mediation. The fundamental question remains: Is ODR safe?

---

30 State of California Commission on Judicial Performance. (n.d.). Judicial misconduct involving bias: Ethnicity, nationality, race, gender and sexual orientation. Retrieved June 13, 2024, from https://cjp.ca.gov/wp-content/uploads/sites/40/2016/08/JUDICIAL-MISCONDUCT-INVOLVING-BIAS-ETHNICITY-NATIONALITY-RACE-GENDER-and-SEXUAL-ORIENTATION.pdf

Trust, fairness, and security are key considerations in the evolution of ODR. Beyond facilitating e-commerce, ODR represents a modern approach to resolving disputes, ranging from family matters to complex civil and commercial cases. The immediacy and interactive capabilities of online platforms enrich the mediation process, enabling participants to engage safely through specialized software designed to protect privacy.

In legal contexts, the efficacy of online conferencing in ensuring secure communications has been well-documented, making it a preferred choice for mediators and lawyers aiming to maintain confidentiality during client interactions and professional collaborations. For example, the DIFC Courts reported significant increases in commercial claims during the first half of 2020, with the Court of First Instance (CFI) experiencing a 96% rise year-on-year. The total value of cases, including arbitration-related matters, reached AED 2.2 billion. Enforcement claims also rose by 15%, totaling AED 192.4 million. The Small Claims Tribunal (SCT) saw 213 claims filed, amounting to AED 24 million. The courts maintained full operational capacity during COVID-19 through enhanced digital infrastructure, issuing over 500 digital Orders and Judgments. Innovations include the region's first e-Registry and a new Arbitration Division to manage increasing arbitration cases efficiently. [31]However, effective utilization of web conferencing apps is crucial to safeguarding privacy, especially amidst global crises like the current pandemic. For instance, Zoom employs robust end-to-end encryption using the AES256 standard for all communications, aligning with stringent privacy standards. Similar encryption measures are available on other platforms, although verifying encryption standards before conducting confidential meetings is advisable.

Despite the benefits, concerns about cybersecurity persist, evidenced by recent incidents of unauthorized access during Zoom meetings, commonly referred to as "Zoom-bombing." To mitigate such risks, legal professionals can secure meetings by locking them once all participants have joined, thereby preventing unauthorized entry even with access credentials. Additionally, alternatives to Zoom, such as Skype for Business and Cisco's WebEx, offer varied features and security protocols, each requiring careful consideration based on encryption capabilities, meeting room security, and user-friendly interfaces.

The advancements in technology have profound implications for mediation, particularly through the emergence of ODR platforms like Cybersettle. These platforms represent a significant evolution in how disputes can be resolved efficiently and effectively without the need for physical presence. One major implication is the increased accessibility of mediation services to parties located in different geographic areas or time zones, overcoming traditional barriers to in-person mediation. This accessibility fosters greater inclusivity and ensures that parties with diverse backgrounds and circumstances can participate in the dispute resolution process.

ODR platforms enhance the speed and convenience of mediation by leveraging technology such as video conferencing, instant messaging, and secure online portals. These tools enable parties to engage in real-time discussions and negotiations, facilitating quicker resolution of disputes compared to traditional methods. For example, in commercial disputes involving international parties, ODR platforms can mitigate logistical challenges and reduce costs associated with travel and accommodation.

These platforms typically operate through several key steps. First, parties register and provide relevant case information online. Second, the platform facilitates communication and negotiation between parties, often through secure messaging or video conferencing features. Third, the parties may use online tools provided by the platform, such as virtual meeting rooms or document sharing capabilities, to exchange information and propose solutions. Throughout this process, a neutral mediator or facilitator may guide the discussions to ensure fairness and adherence to procedural norms.

---

31 DIFC Courts, "DIFC Courts leverages digital infrastructure to accommodate rapid rise in commercial claims," DIFC Courts, Available: https://www.difccourts.ae/media-centre/newsroom/difc-courts-leverages-digital-infrastructure-to-accommodate-rapid-rise-in-commercial-claims

For instance, in a consumer dispute where a buyer and seller are located in different countries, an ODR platform can facilitate mediation sessions via video conferencing, allowing both parties to present their perspectives and negotiate terms of resolution. The platform's secure environment ensures confidentiality and transparency, crucial for maintaining trust in the mediation process. Ultimately, these platforms offer a flexible and efficient alternative to traditional mediation, enabling parties to reach mutually acceptable outcomes while accommodating diverse circumstances and preferences.

7.2 *Cybersecurity and Privacy Concerns*

Cybersecurity and privacy concerns in online mediation are multifaceted and require careful consideration to maintain confidentiality and trust among participants. One critical aspect is the handling of visual and audio data from mediation sessions. It's essential to obtain explicit written consent from all parties before recording or using any such materials to ensure compliance with privacy laws and confidentiality agreements. For example, in a recent online mediation involving sensitive financial information, all parties agreed beforehand on the limited use and storage of digital recordings to protect confidentiality. Another crucial measure is the offline storage of mediation-related documents away from online platforms. This practice ensures that sensitive information, such as evidence or legal documents, remains secure and accessible only to authorized personnel.

The nature of mediation, which involves diverse communication methods, introduces various cybersecurity challenges beyond traditional privacy concerns. These challenges include safeguarding data during transmission, protecting against unauthorized access, and ensuring the integrity of virtual communication channels. For instance, in a cross-border dispute resolution conducted via video conferencing, encryption and secure authentication protocols were implemented to prevent interception and data tampering. Despite these complexities, cybersecurity concerns should not deter the adoption of electronic tools for mediation. Instead, mediators can mitigate risks by implementing robust security protocols, conducting regular risk assessments, and educating all participants on cybersecurity best practices. For example, mediation platforms may offer features such as end-to-end encryption and secure file sharing, enhancing data protection and participant trust.

CHAPTER EIGHT
IMPLEMENTATION OF MEDIATION POLICY AND PROCEDURE

"Peace is not the absence of conflict but the ability to resolve it through peaceful means." — Ronald Reagan

CHAPTER EIGHT: IMPLEMENTATION OF MEDIATION POLICY AND PROCEDURE

1. **The Importance of Mediation Policy and Procedure**

With the use of mediation procedure and skills, employers in the hospitality industry have the perfect imaginative setting when a dispute arises in a non-unionized workplace. The mediation procedure may be produced in an additional policy to the grievance procedure, or it can be a part of the grievance procedure. The skill of a mediator to put out a fire quickly and quietly, leading people directly and openly to discuss their major concerns, earns him/her the reputation of a workplace problem solver that does it now – not later. Positive reputation does not generate revenue overnight. A mediator's reputation to assist the applicable level of authority (last step participation in the grievance process) to solve a problem and the hotel's reputation for caring will evolve through the evolution of different approaches. These approaches include the policy and procedure manual, decisions solved in minutes, hours, or a couple of days.

Employers in the hospitality industry understand that good employees and managers are crucial to a hotel's continued success and positive image. The emphasis in the industry is on providing service and customer satisfaction, and the key to doing so is skilled and experienced employees. Employees in the hospitality industry are also aware of the nature of their work and the relationship with the employer. Because of these employer and employee concerns and the relationship, both players agree that when a problem arises in the workplace, they wish to settle the dispute with a satisfactory solution without interjecting lawyers, collective agreements, or other third parties/specialists into the situation. It is not the intention of either party to escalate the matter and to give the hotel a poor reputation for customer service. Often, employers in the industry incorporate a grievance procedure into their HRs policy, and it is nominally only for unionized employees. This policy is very useful for employees in the industry who are not signatory to a union, and in addition, it sets the scene for switching it up to a mediation policy and procedure when a dispute matures and is not settled.

In addition, the policy should outline the length and cost of a mediation session, the responsibilities of the parties involved in the dispute, the manager's and HR's role, mediation record-keeping, enforcement-of-settlement procedures, and respect for mediation outcomes. Finally, the policy should outline what happens after mediation, i.e., is follow-up needed and in what form. Will feedback be given to the manager about the outcome? Will feedback be given to HR? Will feedback be given to the mediator? If not designated in the policy, these issues should be decided upon in advance of disputes.

2. **Key Components of a Mediation Policy**

The policy should contain step-by-step procedures to aid managers when dealing with disputes. The steps should conform to the types of disputes the parties can sensibly bring to mediation and when they can be brought. It should define key terms and should remind the manager to clarify the source of the problem, e.g., policy breach, unclear instructions or expectations, unresolved issue, and/or personal conflict. The steps in the procedure should be kept simple so that they can be easily understood and quickly applied if the parties responsible for solving the dispute are to be helped. Accompanying guidelines can be more detailed. The policy should also describe the referral process, the mediator selection process, and the role that managers play in mediation.

A. *Designing an Effective Mediation Procedure*

Step 2: Determine the mediation structure. Mediation can be an informal, voluntary procedure. Mediation can be mandatory or only contingent upon certain conditions. When considering a mandatory mediation procedure, ensure that the mediation itself is not the ultimate decision-maker, but rather the ability of the parties to agree to a resolution.

Step 1: Determine who the mediator will be. Mediation can range from the formal meeting in a conference room setting to an individual association or company executive, attorney, or any internal or external person with the ability to facilitate conversation and resolution.

Designing an effective mediation procedure for the hospitality industry takes planning and careful thought. The more effort you put into designing a system on the front end, the more you will save on the back end. It is best to use a trained mediation professional to help you in this process. Following is a step-by-step guide to designing an effective mediation procedure.

I. Initiating the Mediation Process

When mediation is initiated, both parties are given all of the following information in writing:

(a) The name and contact information of the mediation officer and the program manager to discuss the provision of information and support during the mediation process;

(b) Information on the mediation process and procedures, including possible outcomes; and

(c) Instructions for using the mediation process.

As previously mentioned, the mediator does not rule on or impose a solution; rather, the mediator helps to create an independent resolution acceptable to the parties involved. Both parties must agree to mediate, and a mediator will be selected from a list of trained members. A mediator chosen by the disputants serves in guiding them towards their own resolution.

II. Selecting a Mediator

When selecting a mediator, they must be an approved certified mediator from a recognized center, such as the ADR Center certified by the International Mediation Institute (IMI). This ensures the quality of the mediator handling the cases within the organization. Organizations must set a budget for internal candidates who wish to become certified mediators, or they can hire a candidate who already holds such certification. Moreover, organizations can employ external mediators if needed (which will be discussed in the upcoming book) which details the differences between external and internal mediators. However, both internal and external mediators must be certified. The principles of mediation need to be clearly adopted within the organization to report outcomes efficiently in both an academic and practical form, thereby effectively resolving disputes.

Knowledge of mediators can be a key element in selecting a mediator to assist you and the other party in resolving any conflict. It is very important to know the background, training, and experience of any mediator you are considering using. Unfortunately, action or conduct which will allow you to draw many inferences about mediators is very limited. You should ask each mediator for their rules and any guidelines they use in a mediation. It is then left to organization to evaluate such information.

III. Pre-Mediation Preparation

a) Pre-mediation Meeting with the parties, Lawyers or Intermediaries:

The issues to be visited during the pre-mediation meeting with the lawyers, intermediaries, , or parties may include:

- Initial claim report

- Venue/location of the mediation

- Purpose of the meeting

- Identification of the parties

- Provision of necessary preparatory advice

- Detailed discussion of the facts and issues

- Minimum time required

- Pre-mediation documents and any material to be brought to the meeting

- Agreement or restriction to the mediation process

- Safety issue

- Confidentiality

- Warn of any police order or court order, which may cause interruption of the mediation process

Pre-mediation preparation is crucial and should not be underestimated. It may determine the success of the mediation process. For an uncomplicated case, the preparation can take a few minutes to sometimes weeks and months, allowing sufficient time for the mediators to ask questions to each party concerned as well as to conduct some background research on the issue. For complicated cases or matters with a broad history, time constraints may prevent mediators from asking all the questions necessary to prepare sufficiently for the meetings. Insufficient preparation may also result in a late start without identification of the significant issues. Given the possible problems that insufficient preparation may create, the following pre-mediation preparation guide establishes the issues that are relevant in most cases.

IV. *Mediation Session*

Mediation is a flexible process. Neither the mediator nor any of the parties to the dispute can oblige the other party to mediate or to achieve any particular result. If any of the parties does not wish to mediate, achieve a particular result, or pay for services rendered, it is best to reach an agreement between the parties in advance on procedures and costs that might arise. If not, the mediator would decline to take up the matter, except in the very rare cases where the institution has indicated to the mediator that it is willing to meet all its costs.

When both parties to a mediation request agree and ask for it, and the mediator does not consider there to be any particular conflict of interest, the mediation session may also be held in another location to promote better solutions or a better understanding of a different framework of thinking about a problem. This aim can also be addressed by using a format other than the normal one-day mediation if all participants agree.

The mediation session will usually last for one day. Occasionally, where necessary, the session could be extended to reach a good result. It takes place either at the mediator's office or the office of the resolution staff appointed to handle the complaint following a site visit to the institution concerned.

During the mediation sessions, both parties typically have common interests and specific needs that should be identified during the pre-mediation stages and confirmed within the mediation session itself. Understanding these needs is crucial to determining the structure of the mediation, whether it will involve joint sessions, separate sessions, or a combination of both.

In some cases, parties may become frustrated during joint sessions, potentially leading to a breakdown in communication. To mitigate this, the mediator must consistently remind the parties of the confidentiality agreement in place and their role as a facilitator aimed at helping them reach a settlement. The mediator should also highlight the common interests shared by the parties, such as the desire to maintain or extend their relationship.

At the beginning of the mediation sessions, these are the typical concerns: establishing the interests and needs of each party, deciding the format of the sessions, and ensuring that all participants are reminded of the ground rules and objectives. This approach helps create a constructive environment where the mediator can guide the parties toward a mutually beneficial resolution.

V. *Opening Statements*

The opening statement is more apt to succeed if it avoids any "sales pitch." People coming to the mediation are not attending to hear about your 98% success rate in resolving similar disputes. Many mediators feel that the parties will go away and think about their opening statement. The mediators make the point that it can be more effective to deal with any comfort zone issues during the joint meeting or caucus.

I suggest that you start by introducing the participants and explaining who they are. It is good to use a flip-chart for this so the parties can visualize who they are. People usually say, "You can introduce me when the disputing parties arrive," but they might change their mind when they arrive because introducing parties is a psychological link for the participants. They will make eye contact, and in so doing, the process has started.

The opening statement is the start of your mediation. It is how you open the communication channel and create a connection between you and the disputing parties. This is an important task and when done effectively, it will put the parties at ease and show them that you are someone worth listening to.

Example of an Opening Statement:

"Good morning, everyone. My name is Mohamed Darwish and I will be your mediator today. I'd like to start by thanking you all for being here and committing to this process. Today, our goal is to work together to find a mutually agreeable solution to the issues at hand. Before we begin, I want to introduce everyone in the room. [Participant A], [Participant B], could you briefly introduce yourselves and your roles?

I also want to explain that our sessions are confidential, and nothing said here can be used outside this room. My role is to facilitate the conversation, ensure that everyone is heard, and help you navigate towards a resolution. I am not here to make decisions for you but to assist you in finding common ground. Let's start by discussing the main issues that brought you here today."

Explaining the mediator's role as a facilitator rather than a decision-maker manages expectations and clarifies that the session's goal is to find common ground. Without this introduction, the mediation might lack structure, increase tension, and lead to misunderstandings about the mediator's role and the session's purpose. By providing a clear agenda, such as outlining that each party will give an overview of their perspective, identify key areas of agreement and disagreement, and work on solutions, the mediator creates a roadmap that encourages participation and facilitates agreement. Thus, an effective opening statement is essential for building trust, setting expectations, and providing a framework for discussions, making it a critical component for a successful resolution.

VI. *Information Sharing*

In the process of discussing with the parties, the mediator needs to establish rapport with the parties. The mediator's role is not to provide answers, but to help disputing parties. The purpose of the mediator's repeating, rephrasing, or reflecting the party's message is to enhance the party's perception of the other party's or the mediator's understanding. Such reflection presents no judgment, then, but merely assurance of the listener's understanding. If delays are encountered due to non-cooperation and the delicacy of the mediation dynamics, the mediator may have to seek permission to meet separately without breach of confidentiality.

The inquiry phase helps the mediator to gain an understanding of the problems and issues under the dispute and appreciate the positions and interests of the parties. In this phase, the mediator will spend more time talking to the parties. The mediator must ensure that the conversation is conducted impartially and in the presence of the other party if he is available. The mediator will show an interest in the party's perspectives about the issues and the significant underlying interests and needs, which it appears to the party. They should elicit the understanding of past conduct and any direct or third-party communications to date, paying particular attention to commonly requested documents.

B. *Training and Education for Mediators*

Training should be integrated with also educating management in preventive, pre-existing mediation, and ADR systems. The purpose of the latter is to encourage hotel and lodging managers to create an organizational culture that not only understands and uses grassroots ADR but also develops an insatiable desire to teach it. At the same time, managers must have an obligation to develop a relationship with a mediation service, recognizing the long-term benefits of utilizing a broad-based mediation service solutions approach. To take maximum advantage, a neutral must have the ability to tailor and tweak training to management's level of sophistication, using practical case studies with industry-specific educational material. Be clear. The purpose of a hospitality/hotel management program is not intended to create or develop mediators or area resorts students but to educate industry managers with the ADR playbook available for application to disputes among employees or with guests.

Training and education in mediation procedure, policy, and practice should be provided by industry experts and professionals who are specially trained in the art of mediation. The service should include a curriculum created according to industry best standards. The mediation service should have access to sophisticated training technology. Accomplished, respected, and senior practitioners should deliver the hands-on training. Training is essential in teaching hospitality and lodging mediation to be grounded in understanding the institutional details that exist in the specifics of the lodging industry.

3. **Legal Considerations in Mediation Policies**

The support personnel could be anyone who has the interests and/or concerns of the employee in attendance in the mediation session. The presence of a legal representative is not always required, it is up to the employee's discretion. The things covered in the mediation sessions must remain confidential, but it is noted that an individual present at a mediation session could be summoned by a court to testify regarding a dispute that was being addressed at the mediation session, destroying any confidentiality. It is important for all individuals at the mediation session to adhere to the company rules and instructions, and to be respectful to all participants. All parties should seek the guidance and understanding of the Mediator, to make sure that all individuals are heard. The Mediator will maintain order and control of the session, conduct the opening statements, and verify the attendees' understanding of the confidentiality principle of the session and, most importantly, maintain a neutral position - not weighing in on the specific disputes or opinions about the dispute, but fostering understanding and seeking wise choices for resolution.

It is important that the language in the internal policies be clear, concise, and relevant to the business of the hospitality industry. It is important to remember that employees are not attorneys and will have no working knowledge of interpreting contract language written within the policy, nor should they. Therefore, precise language is essential. Following are some legal terms frequently written into mediation policies and procedures, and how the terms are often enforced within mediation. Employees should be encouraged to bring support personnel of their choice to the mediation session. The term referred should be previously defined in the employment manual policies, i.e., co-worker, peer, subordinate, union representative, attorney, etc. The support personnel of their choice could be an attorney, family or personal representative, union representative, or other monitor, any individual who supports the employee. Individuals at the mediation session are not required to be present for the whole session but should be prepared to participate if their names are referred to during the course of the session.

4. **Measuring the Effectiveness of Mediation Policies**

Measuring the effectiveness of mediation policies. Often, simply having an effective policy in place is not enough. Other steps must be taken if the policy is going to be effective. And the first step is determining just how well a mediation program does what it is supposed to. The traditional methods of ADR policy "meeting" the needs of a company are not accurate enough. These subjective measurements say little about how cost-effective a program is or how good an outcome policy provides. Policy goals pertaining to employer-employee relations and the organization's public image are similarly deficient. A serious program would include measuring the effects of the policy as a way to verify its effectiveness.

To ensure that a mediation policy is truly effective, it's crucial to establish rigorous evaluation methods that assess its real-world impact. Evaluating the outcomes of mediation policies systematically allows organizations to validate their effectiveness and pinpoint areas needing enhancement. Key aspects to consider when evaluating the effectiveness of a mediation policy include:

1. **Cost Savings Analysis**: This involves conducting a thorough examination of the costs associated with implementing the mediation policy compared to traditional dispute resolution methods like litigation or arbitration. It includes quantifying expenses such as mediator fees, administrative costs, legal fees, and the time spent by employees on dispute resolution. By comparing these costs, organizations can determine if mediation is a more cost-effective approach.

2. **Employee Satisfaction Surveys**: Employee satisfaction is a crucial indicator of the success of a mediation policy. Surveys or interviews can be conducted to gather feedback from employees who have participated in mediation sessions. Questions can cover various aspects such as the ease of access to mediation services, satisfaction with the mediator's skills and neutrality, perceived fairness of the process, and overall satisfaction with the outcomes. Analyzing this feedback provides insights into the effectiveness of the mediation policy in meeting the needs and expectations of employees.

3. **Online Reviews on Google, TripAdvisor, and Booking.com**: Monitoring online reviews on platforms like Google, TripAdvisor, and Booking.com can serve as valuable KPIs for assessing the impact of mediation on guest satisfaction and reputation management. Guests often share their experiences with dispute resolution processes in online reviews, providing candid feedback on the effectiveness of mediation in addressing their concerns. Organizations can track the frequency and sentiment of reviews related to dispute resolution to gauge the perceived effectiveness of their mediation policies. Positive reviews praising efficient and satisfactory resolution demonstrate the success of mediation efforts, while negative reviews highlighting unresolved issues or dissatisfaction signal areas for improvement.

4. **Resolution Time frame Assessment**: Tracking the time taken to resolve disputes through mediation is essential for assessing its efficiency. Organizations can compare the average resolution time

for mediated cases with that of cases resolved through traditional methods. Shorter resolution time frames indicate that mediation is a more efficient approach to resolving disputes, reducing downtime and allowing parties to move forward more quickly.

5. **Recurrence of Disputes Analysis**: Monitoring the recurrence of disputes involving the same parties or similar issues after mediation provides valuable insights into the long-term effectiveness of the mediation policy. A decrease in the frequency of repeated disputes suggests that mediation is successful in addressing underlying issues and preventing future conflicts. This analysis helps organizations understand the extent to which mediation contributes to sustainable conflict resolution and relationship-building.

6. **Data Collection and Analysis**: Collecting and analyzing relevant data is essential for evaluating the overall impact of the mediation policy. Organizations should systematically gather data on cost savings, employee satisfaction levels, resolution time frames, and dispute recurrence rates. By analyzing this data over time, organizations can identify trends, patterns, and areas for improvement in their mediation processes.

7. **Continuous Improvement Initiatives**: Based on the insights gained from data analysis and feedback from stakeholders, organizations can implement continuous improvement initiatives to enhance their mediation policies further. This may involve refining mediation procedures, providing additional training for mediators, addressing common challenges identified through feedback, or updating mediation policies based on evolving organizational needs and best practices in conflict resolution.

By implementing these mechanisms and continuously evaluating and improving their mediation policies, organizations within the hospitality industry can create more effective and efficient conflict resolution processes that promote a positive workplace environment and contribute to long-term organizational success.

5. Confidentiality and Ethics

As previously mentioned, mediators must be free from conflicts of interest. If a mediator is also employed by an organization that may or may not be involved in the dispute, this mediator must disclose this fact at the outset to the parties to the dispute, and one of the other mediators must take the lead in managing the mediation process. Furthermore, some organizations have ethics rules that require disclosure of private interests. If mediators are subject to any rules that govern ethical behaviour, these rules must also be adhered to. In general, mediators must act with honesty, fairness, sensitivity, and competence. The chief goal of a mediator is to assist the parties, not to promote his or her own personal interests or that of any other organization.

Confidentiality is an essential element of an effective mediation program. All individuals involved in the mediation process must agree to respect the confidentiality of the mediation proceeding and its outcome. Confidentiality means that all discussions and/or documents prepared specifically for the mediation are private and will not be repeated or used in a formal judicial or administrative proceeding. If mediation participants do not abide by the principles of confidentiality, they may be subject to penalties, including possible exclusion from the formal legal/administrative proceedings pertaining to the dispute. Confidentiality encourages open and candid communication among the participants and the mediators. Parties tend to compromise better when they can trust the process and the mediator.

The actual mechanics of implementing a confidentiality clause, on the other hand, contribute to confusion among participants. Most often, the underlying tension surfaces when a legislator proposes passing a statute or a regulator a rule that specifically mandates that certifiably non-confidential records be made of what transpires, even though the process is otherwise designed to produce a non-confidential resolution. The basis for respect for confidentiality, with relative public and private immunities for mediator performance, is rooted in at least two areas of law, both complex and not amenable to instant clarification.

There is consensus in the ADR field that confidentiality is one of its hallmarks and is an essential feature of any mediation policy. Ambiguity, misunderstanding, and variation in practices and expectations, however, have prompted private and public organizations designing mediation policies to spell out their protection to establish uniform, consistent expectations, and to add clout and compelling power to the policy. Different organizations achieve this end by deploying varying words, phrases, and clauses.

6. Conclusion and Future Trends

In conclusion, despite the limited adoption of mediation policies and procedures within the hospitality industry, this book serves as a catalyst for initiating crucial discussions and considerations among hospitality management stakeholders. The aim is to shed light on the potential benefits that the implementation of such policies can offer. Traditionally, the hospitality sector has relied heavily on conventional conflict resolution methods, such as litigation or arbitration, often resulting in prolonged disputes, increased costs, and strained relationships. However, by introducing mediation as an alternative approach, there is an opportunity to transform the landscape of dispute resolution within the industry.

One of the key objectives of this initiative is to encourage stakeholders to recognize mediation as a viable and effective means of addressing conflicts in the hospitality sector. Mediation offers a collaborative and solution-focused approach, wherein parties have the opportunity to actively participate in the resolution process, preserving relationships, and fostering mutual understanding. Unlike traditional adversarial methods, mediation promotes open communication, creativity, and flexibility, allowing for tailored solutions that meet the specific needs and interests of all parties involved.

Moreover, by embracing mediation, the hospitality industry can benefit from various advantages, including cost savings, time efficiency, and enhanced guest satisfaction. Mediation can significantly reduce the time and resources expended on lengthy legal proceedings, enabling parties to reach resolutions swiftly and effectively. Additionally, the confidential nature of mediation safeguards sensitive information and reputations, mitigating potential damage to the brand and preserving the goodwill of the parties involved.

Furthermore, by embracing mediation, hospitality management stakeholders can cultivate a culture of proactive conflict resolution and collaboration within their organizations. Implementing mediation policies not only equips employees with valuable conflict resolution skills but also demonstrates a commitment to fostering a supportive and harmonious work environment. This proactive approach can contribute to improved employee morale, retention, and overall organizational performance.

Overall, this book aims to spark a paradigm shift in the hospitality industry by advocating for the widespread adoption of mediation policies and procedures. Through proactive engagement and dialogue, stakeholders can collectively explore the potential benefits of mediation and work towards integrating it into the fabric of their organizations. By embracing mediation as a preferred method of conflict resolution, the hospitality sector can unlock new opportunities for growth, innovation, and sustainable relationship management, ultimately paving the way for a more resilient and thriving industry landscape.

"I may have added the knowledge I obtained along the years and I was hoping to convey something from what I gained and learned to you and to the next generations, disputes have always existed since the creation of the universe, but whoever can resolve conflicts amicably is the one who gains the trust and the hearts of others.

This message is for you, every one of us reaches the station of life at different time and will leave the train at different time as well. All that will remain is your reputation which will leave a legacy in the hearts of those you encountered during your Journey.

In the end, be good to everyone, respect everyone. Everyone is fighting his or her own battle and everyone has his or her own examination paper, not everyone having the same questions and therefore there is no definite answers.

Enjoy the journey of your life and make it a Journey of Harmony"

Add your notes here and in the upcoming pages.